Camouflaged Love

A Memoir

Lorin R. Hayes

Those wishing to contact Lorin Hayes may do so at the following:
www.lorinhayes.com
or
Heart 4 Hope LLC
1821 N. Lake Forest Dr. 700-315
McKinney, Texas 75071

All rights reserved No part of this book may be reproduced or transmittted in any form or by any means, electronic or mechanical, including photocopying and recording, or by any information storage and retrieval system without prior permission in writing from the publisher.

The author of this book does not dispense medical advice or prescribe the use of any technique as a form of treatment for physical, mental or emotional health without the advice of a medical professional either directly or indirectly.

Some minor details and names have been changed in order to protect the identities of the persons involved.

Published in the United States by Heart 4 Hope LLC, Texas.

ISBN paperback: 978-1-7375207-0-2
ISBN ebook: 978-1-7375207-1-9

Library of Congress Control Number: 2021913209.

Cover design: Stephen Hayes
Author Photo: Lauren Bier Photography

For my loving husband,
and for the women who have served our country.

Contents

Prologue	vi
1 Journey's Start	1
2 New Duty Station	7
3 Stalker	17
4 Caribbean Blues	22
5 Seasons Change	37
6 First Impression to Lasting Impression	44
7 Chapel Duty and Extra Duty	51
8 The Eagle has landed	58
9 Grief	66
10 Falling	71
11 Family Visits	75
12 Fraternizing	80
13 Unconventional Dating	85
14 Paradise	92
15 Sleeping Arrangements	98
16 Intel	103
17 The Exodus	108

18 New York State of Mind	113
19 She's White	122
20 Ring in the New Year	131
21 Friendly Fire	137
22 Welcome to the Infantry	144
23 Female Soldier	151
24 JAG	158
25 Whistleblower	165
26 Paperwork	173
27 Wedding Invite Fright	180
28 Wedding Day	187
29 Back Up	195
30 To Reenlist or Not Reenlist?	204
31 Farewells and Forgiveness	216
Epilogue	224
Acknowledgements	227
Resources	230
Author Bio	234

Prologue

Imagine that you are peacefully sleeping, when suddenly a police squad comes busting through the door, SWAT style, and flies into your house. They drag you out of your bed in the middle of the night. Meanwhile, your sleeping children wake up. Frightened in the next room, they can hear their parents being arrested. Wait, did you kill someone? It has to be something big! What crime did you commit?

However crazy this scenario sounds, this is an authentic story, but it's not my story. This is the reality for Mildred and Richard Loving. The Lovings were a couple in the late sixties who had broken the law by marrying interracially. Their story is a source of inspiration to continue to fight for what is right, noble, and just. It sparks passion not only for my own interracial relationship, but for justice for others. In the case *Loving vs. Virginia*, the police arrested them, jailed them, kicked them out of their home, and banned them from the state of Virginia. They were told their marriage was neither legitimate nor recognized in the

Prologue

Commonwealth of Virginia.*

    In school, we learned about the civil rights movement, but it seemed so far away, so foreign, so out of touch with my reality. Portrayed in its black and white print and video, the civil rights fight seemed like ancient history. History lessons glorified a society as being evolved enough to realize the painful history of our country. The vast message received was the mistreatment of minorities, especially of African Americans, as something so far removed, so barbaric and shameful, and uncomfortable. The unspoken message was to vaguely acknowledge it and move on. That part of history is over, right?

    No.

    The injustices thrust upon the lives of people in minority groups are not things we can wrap up and tie with a pretty bow. It's a much more complicated, painful, and pervasive issue than most realize. The effects of inequality are woven into our lives, seen or unseen. As a friend, and then more intimately as a wife, I have walked beside others and witnessed racism up close and personal. It plays into the backgrounds of all of our collective lives. The start of the official civil rights movement is maybe one or two generations removed from most. However, today, we still see news displaying basic rights violated continuously for African Americans and other minority groups.

---

* Library of Congress. https://www.loc.gov/item/usrep388001 (accessed May 15, 2020).

CAMOUFLAGED LOVE

The Lovings dealt with far more than I can ever imagine. I cannot comprehend staying quiet and living in a society with its citizens being in constant fear that harm could befall their families. Death threats, physical and verbal assaults, jail time, and fear for the safety and wellbeing of one's family should never be normalized.

My journey is one through discovery, expectations, prejudices, and racism, a coming of age, as well as forgiveness, all wrapped up in a love story. It's one of finding my voice, finding people for me, questioning, and deepening my faith. I hope that my story may inspire others to stand up for justice and to encourage that there can be beauty made from the ashes of our lives.

Chapter One

Journey's Start

The wind swept down from the majestic snowcapped mountains, to toss my sandy blonde hair, swirling around my face. I brushed it back and tucked it behind my ears and blinked hard in the rays of light, continuing down the sidewalk toward my future, as my pink suitcase clunked behind me. It was a gorgeous day in May. It was warmer in my hometown, but the lovely surroundings and the smell in the crisp air reminded me of grass, as well as oak and pine trees, towers among the smaller mountains and hills nestled near where I spent most of my childhood in upstate New York. I was born in the city, but my family spent the summers and weekends camping near Woodstock, made famous for peace, love, and rock and roll. When I was in the fourth grade, we packed up and moved to the sticks—from Brooklyn to the suburbs, to the Catskills.

I enjoyed doing new things, and this—this was an adventure.

"Yes! That's it. Look at it as an adventure," I whispered to myself. I was not used to being this far away from home. Granted, I had spent the last summer on a mission trip in Brazil, yet I had an end to that trip, and here I had signed my life away. I filled out a dream sheet while I was waiting in AIT (Advanced Individual Training) to train as a chaplain assistant in the Army. A dream sheet was a list of three potential stateside assignments and three potential overseas duty stations that a soldier preferred.

What did I put down on the top of my list for the overseas assignments? Hawaii. Yet here I was at my first Army duty station, the dual Army and Air Force base in Anchorage, Alaska. I thought that it must be some kind of cruel joke. I asked for tropical warmth, sun-kissed skin, tranquil blue waves breaking on the shore, and I imagined squishing sand in my toes and palm trees leaning in the breeze. Instead, they sent me to the tundra. My mind mulled over the words of my instructors. They were echoing in my ear.

"Well, at least it's not Fort Wainwright. Fort Wainwright is in Fairbanks, and that is in the middle of nowhere. At least there is plenty to do in Anchorage."

Anchorage was a major city in Alaska, with nightlife, restaurants, malls, activities, and easy access to flights to the other states. I took a few breaths as I approached the barracks they assigned me to. I opened the door and realized I had a roommate.

"Hi! I'm Tee," She welcomed me and then plopped down on the chair in the kitchenette.

"So how do you feel about Alaska so far? It's beautiful, right?" she asked.

She had me there. It was breathtaking. I shifted my weight to lean against the wall.

"Well… yes. It's gorgeous, but I wanted to go to Hawaii. I put that on my wish list," I replied.

"Well, even though we are far away from our families here in Alaska, at least there are things to do and places to go here. It could be worse. You could be at the other Army installation in Fairbanks. Now *that* is the middle of nowhere, and the weather is extreme there, too! Anchorage doesn't get colder than maybe thirty below. Fairbanks has brutal winters. I heard it can get to be seventy-five degrees below in the winter in Fairbanks. Count yourself lucky!"

She invited me to spend the weekend with her friends at a barbecue on the Air Force side. The Air Force had newer, more pristine barracks and more amenities. Even the DFAC (dining facility) on the Air Force side had better food. You could leave your tray after you ate, and the workers took your tray and clean up after you. Talk about service! Since basic training in the Army, I had to clear off my own trays and hand them in, like a school lunchroom. A girl could get used to this!

I easily became friends with Tee and her group of friends. The weekend had me settling into my new normal. Waking up to the mountains each day and the fresh outdoor air made me smile. I enjoyed a delicious spread of authentic Jamaican food cooked by Tee's friend's cousin and their group of friends. They were fun-loving, and my belly hurt from laughing at the stories they told, and we danced to music as they cooked.

I liked my unit, my room, and the friends I made. Anchorage was growing on me. On Sunday, I went to the movies with Tee, and my body felt light, and I even skipped a little, poking fun at Tee.

"So when are you going to tell him you like him? I saw how you looked at your 'friend.'"

There was obviously some chemistry between her and one of the guys in the group. I felt as if I had known Tee for years, and I was grateful for such a quick friendship.

"Tee, you know, I'm actually kind of glad I didn't get stationed in Hawaii. It's beautiful here, and my instructor from the chaplain schoolhouse even called because my sergeant asked what I did to get a call vouching for me?"

I smiled, reminiscing about the silliest thing I had gotten hemmed up for. I snuck contraband in to the barracks during training. I had a sweet tooth, and I felt that I deserved to take some sweets to the barracks. I remember the look on Sergeant Whisk's face when I told him I didn't have the receipt (I had thrown out the evidence), and my pockets in my uniform bulged with my contraband. I was a terrible deceiver, and he raised his eyebrow and told me he wasn't buying it. I told that lie, with a shifty gaze, but as he scanned my uniform and noticed my pockets and pointed to them, I cracked.

"Okay, so I didn't lose it. I threw out my receipt because I really wanted these gummy worms!"

I scooped them out of my pockets and into his hands. I felt like a kid who had been caught sneaking a cookie. I was so upset, not that I had gotten caught, but that I had let him down. I had made it my mission to prove my worthiness and honor and that I earned back the trust and respect of my leaders.

When Monday rolled around, I briefly met with some chaplain assistants at morning formation. So far they had been so kind to me, and it started to feel like Anchorage was growing on me. I fit in here.

Over the next few days, I brought my orders around and continued with the administrative and logistical part of being new. Traveling back and forth across many buildings on post, I hummed to myself as I

Journey's Start

checked off all the boxes, walking to all the tan buildings that all looked the same—cold and sterile. The only difference seemed to be the number on the outside of the building.

I smiled and imagined what Alaskan adventures were ahead, including whale watching and glacier climbing. I was ready for it. I had just handed in all my medical and dental records to the medical facility, when a fellow soldier from my unit scurried up.

"Hey, First Sergeant wants to see you now!"

I gulped. I had been here less than a week and just had started to make friends, but I had done nothing to warrant getting into any trouble!

I made the journey back to the unit. I stood in front of the opened door of the first sergeant's office, the door ajar. My mind started racing over the possibilities. What did I do wrong? I must have messed up the paperwork or something, and I thought he was going to chew me out and call me a soup sandwich, which is fancy Army lingo to say you are a hot mess, to tell you how like an earthworm you are, and make you shrink to the size of an ant.

"First Sergeant, you wanted to see me?" I shrank away from the open door.

"Come in, PFC Whiteman." (Yes, that was my last name, and yes, I know the *White Men Can't Jump* movie reference). "I'm sorry, but it looks like we won't be working with you here. You have direct orders to Fort Wainwright, Alaska."

My voice cracked, "What do you mean, First Sergeant? Did I do something wrong?"

"No, and I tried to fight for you to stay. God knows we need the spot filled. Your AIT instructor called me, so I know you must have done something right, but it's out of my hands."

I had just started to feel settled there, and I loved my new friends and life.

"Go back and pick up your medical and dental records, and turn in anything issued by the company now. Your plane leaves tomorrow."

I mustered, "Yes, First Sergeant," as my shoulders dropped. I closed the door behind me.

Dread filled my body, and I tried to walk straight, but my legs felt like noodles. All the comments came rushing back.

"At least it's not Fort Wainwright. That place is the worst. I would hate to get stuck there."

After I collected my thoughts, I called my mom to tell her the bad news. She tried to reassure me that I would be okay. As I got off the phone with my mom, I sobbed and felt sorry for myself. I said goodbye to Tee, and when night rolled around, I drifted off to sleep, knots twisted in my stomach, and I wished I could go back home.

Chapter 2

New Duty Station

I stepped off the plane with a pit in my stomach. I used the USO to call the number for my new chain of command at Fort Wainwright. Thirty minutes later, the unit sent my NCO (noncommissioned officer) to pick me up from the airport. He was in his mid to late thirties. He felt that women were weak and emotional and had no place in any branch in the military. He was quite the charmer… just kidding. His disdain for me was apparent. As he tossed my suitcase in the back of his truck, he made sure I knew how much of an inconvenience I was to him and to other soldiers. Frankly, I wasn't too fond of him either.

Constructed during the WWII era, the barracks outside looked like most of the other buildings on post, cream and weathered on the outside. Inside, there was a long corridor with tan, brown, and eggshell colored walls that were textured, somewhat tan floors that had been white at one time, but due to their age, had grown tattered looking. It was a three-story building, with the front facing the street and sidewalk. On the backside of the building was the paved parking lot and gravel. The barracks hallway had a cold, sterile feel, like a hospital. The floors gleamed with the wax laid on it by extra duty soldiers, who got in trouble for God only knows what. Along the hallways were all the barracks rooms in a row. The soldiers shared bathrooms on each level. There was a female and male bathroom at the end of the hall that had four shower stalls and four bathroom stalls for the three wings of rooms on each floor.

In my room, I discovered a folded, itchy, forest green wool blanket and some white, starchy sheets. I threw my pink fleece down, shoved the wool blanket in the dresser, and became friends with my bilingual neighbor, Danica. Her glossy chestnut hair flowed to the middle of her petite frame. Her hazel eyes were as warm as her disposition. She was both kind and hilarious. Danica spent a good deal of time on her phone with her husband. He was also in the Army but had moved to another duty station in another state.

My direct supervisor was better than my old-fashioned sergeant and received her promotion the night before I arrived. She was gorgeous with warm chestnut eyes, with micro-braided hair down to her shoulders and a bright smile. She exuded confidence, in starch contrast to me: clumsy, unsure, and stumbling in an unfamiliar place. Sergeant Tiger lived diagonally across the hall from me and graciously started giving me rides to work. I didn't have a car, and since we worked at the same place, clear across base, she allowed me to carpool with her. She was very particular about her new white car, and I had to clank my boots together precisely three times before getting into her car, which was okay. Everyone has their things. Mine is a sink full of dishes—I can't stand it.

As time passed, something shifted.

Sergeant Tiger stopped me in the hall on the way to the bathroom or knock on my door to discuss my whereabouts.

New Duty Station

"I heard your door open and close at 10 P.M. Where were you going?" Her eyes accused me of whatever she had concocted in her mind.

"Um, the latrine, Sergeant."

Consumed with knowing what I was doing, even if I was off duty, she kept tabs on me.

"I heard you were talking to so-and-so," and, "I heard you went to the movies with this soldier," and again, "My sources saw you together, laughing with that soldier."

Part of me felt as if she was trying to be my big sister, but the other part of me believed it was something else. Being fresh meat at a new duty station meant I was the topic of many conversations. It becomes a contest of sorts—that everybody wants to talk to you, date you, or sleep with you. It may be that the guy she liked was trying to get with me, or he hurt her feelings. I could never figure out what it was, but she wasn't pleased with me. On one particular occasion, while I was talking to one of the male sergeants in my unit, Sergeant Tiger crossed her arms, stepped in front of me, and redirected the conversation, so it was all about her. I hadn't the foggiest idea if they had a past together, but I wasn't trying to date him. I was just trying to make friends.

In my limited experience of dating in my life, I was awkward. Heck, I didn't have my first kiss until I was almost seventeen. My dating skills consisted of what I had learned from my friends and on TV. I always thought about dating as figuring out if the person was compatible or if he had the potential of being a husband. I was very purposeful, at that point, in dating only people if they were looking for a relationship that could develop into a serious one, and, eventually, marriage. Some friends from home called me an old soul, and some called me old-fashioned, but I was not interested in dating just for fun. I had this timeline for my life, and I did not want any distractions to where I knew I was going.

CAMOUFLAGED LOVE

When I arrived in Alaska, I had a boyfriend and had no qualms with making that known. Female and male soldiers alike kept telling me that long-distance relationships don't last, and, sooner or later, I was single. I shook my head and said no. However, a few weeks after I arrived, their predictions became accurate. I called him a few weeks after I had been in Fairbanks. I was sad and lonely, and the four-hour time difference and the waiting around for phone calls were depressing. I had tried before I had left, but I chickened out. I said to myself, "Here goes nothing." I swallowed hard, listening to the phone ring, jiggling my leg and holding my breath.

"Hello! How's the Army life treating you? Did you build an igloo yet?" his excited voice asked.

"Um, Hi," I nervously replied.

"What's wrong? You sound down. Is everything okay?"

"No. Not really. Listen. We need to talk."

"That's never a good thing. Let's talk about something else for now. So, guess what I did this weekend? Oh, and you will never believe…"

"I know you don't want to talk about it, and I know you know what I am going to say, but we have to talk about it. I think we should break up. I am really sorry, and I know this isn't the best way for someone to break up with another person, but I can't string you along for another six months or more until I can see you face to face to tell you."

"Don't do this. We can make it work," he pleaded.

"I'm sorry. I tried to tell you before I left that it's just not realistic. We are in two different places, and you can't change my mind. I'm so sorry. I don't mean to hurt you."

"Please! Don't do this. We can make it work," he begged.

New Duty Station

"I'm so sorry. I'm sorry that this hurts you. I'm sorry. I have to go."

I hung up my phone quickly, feeling guilty, as he still protested. I didn't mean to hurt his feelings, but I didn't feel as if I had another option. My neighbors must have overheard some of the conversation, thanks to our paper-thin walls and speakerphone, because the word spread quickly.

My neighbor across the hall was three inches taller than my five-foot-four-inch frame. Jay was a firefighter. He wore his hat backwards, and we liked a lot of the same music. His speakers always crooned a little soul, R&B, the modern John Legend, and my favorites from the 60s, like Al Green, and the notes danced across the hall to my room. He sipped on his coronas as he spent his off time painting amazing replicas of famous paintings and photos, such as the picture of a firefighter kneeling in front of the rumble of 9/11. He always greeted me with, "Hey Whiteman. How are you doing today?"

My two neighbors told me many people left their door open if they were home, so their friends could drop by and hang out if they wanted. Barracks are like college dorms. I met most of the peers in my unit this way.

One of these peers to include was a soldier who shot off his own trigger finger, so he wouldn't have to deploy. Another was a self-proclaimed cowboy, looking for an amiable country girl who loved country music (spoiler alert, that wasn't me). I guess one look at my florescent skin, and I was all "figured out." To be honest, isn't that how most people are? We make snap judgments about people based on appearances? Regardless, I wasn't into country music or him.

I spent the majority of my first few months trying to make friends. I tried desperately with the few females in my unit—there were only eight women. Some ignored me or gave dirty looks, and some just didn't engage me beyond saying hello.

The military is dominated by male soldiers, but in Fairbanks, the ratio was something like ten males to every female. So, women were a hot commodity and could bask in the attention. Too much of that attention made my cheeks and ears rouge. I wanted to be seen, but not that much. I was a shy cheerleader in high school. I loved the dancing and the competitions, but I preferred to hide toward the back, avoiding being the center of attention. I always wanted to be a part of a team, but I was uncomfortable with all the eyes on me.

Although I had fun just being friends with the guys, rumors started flying. Anytime I talked to someone of the opposite sex, a new rumor spread. I had not even considered anyone romantically yet, but they labeled me as "easy." Rumors spread that I was sleeping with any guy who talked to me. God forbid I went out to the movies with someone or went to grab some food! I then was hated, shunned, and dismissed by not only the females in my unit, but all the females in the barracks, who cut their eyes at me.

I caught on that this was the case and became less conversational and shied away from being too friendly with any guy, out of fear of them misconstruing my kindness and spreading any more rumors. I automatically blushed if a guy talked to me because it was attention and it usually made me uncomfortable, and the glares from my surroundings overwhelmed me. I gazed at the groups that joked together, longing to join in, looking away when someone caught my eye.

The thought that no one wanted to befriend me, for me, made me sink back into my shell.

I had always prided myself on my reputation. In high school I was voted "Most Friendly." I saw myself as a kind, caring person, and I wanted to be liked by others. As a Christian, I tried to hold myself to a standard. I wasn't always perfect, but I was always striving to do better, and

New Duty Station

honor was very important to me. For this reason, I started to withdraw from the few guy friends that I had. I didn't want them to misinterpret me, and I didn't want the other females in my unit to misinterpret my intentions. For a few weeks, I wallowed in self-pity, longing to find my place. Maybe I could make just one friend? I was "in processing" into the unit, so for a few weeks I didn't do much socializing besides seeing my unit at morning and evening formation. I handed in paperwork and went to different stations to integrate into Alaska life, to include receiving TA-50 snow gear, filling out paperwork, etc., before my job began.

Early one morning during physical training, while the first sergeant was yelling at our company to stay in formation for the run, running the umpteenth mile during our morning exercise, I glanced sideways and locked eyes with another female soldier in the unit. We gave each other that "I'm over it" look, and I laughed. After catching our breaths after PT, we walked together toward our barracks and the shared bathroom. She had smooth brown skin, with piercing russet eyes, short curly coils, and an infectious laugh.

"I can't stand, and these runs…" she sighed.

I nodded in agreement.

"It's the worst!" Her voice sounded so familiar to me.

"Wait… where are you from?" I asked

"New York."

"Me too! What part?"

"Queens," she replied.

"Oh! My grandparents live in Queens. I was born in Brooklyn but spent most of my childhood in upstate New York!"

"Do you want to come with me to get breakfast?" she asked.

"Sure!"

Over the hate of Army runs and love of food, we hit it off. All a person really needs is one loyal friend, someone who is always there for you. The Bible says a brother is born for times of adversity. Kay helped me feel as if I mattered, that I could do this whole "Army thing" and make friends. She was laid back and honest, and she took me under her wing. We had fun hanging out, going out to eat, and visiting the Enlisted Club on base that held dances, such as salsa nights. We even had a girl's trip with Sergeant Tiger to a beautiful log cabin in the town of Denali, overlooking the Denali mountain peak, the highest mountain peak in North America. We shopped together at the eight-store mall, got our nails done, and watched movies. She hugged me when I was down. She listened to me and encouraged me. I could glance her way, and we could roll our eyes and have an entire conversation with our faces about the ridiculousness of the Army's "hurry up and wait" theme.

Over time, I became friends with my neighbor, Danica, and became an acquaintance with my neighbor, Sergeant Jay. Jay was a non-commissioned officer who had gotten in trouble for a DUI. He surprised me by quoting Bible verses and confessed that he used to be a man of faith, but he said he had lost faith because of the horrendous things he had seen when he deployed. During his off time, there was seldom a time to find him without a drink in his hand. To be fair, most soldiers drank, some excessively, during the weekend, continually. I believed he drank, just as other veterans had told me, to deal with the images of the war he had seen and what he went through—a story that is all too common in people I have met over the years.

Since Sergeant Jay had a DUI, he could not legally drive.

"Could you drive my car to help me get some errands done?"

New Duty Station

I nodded, and spent a couple of hours driving around town to do grocery shopping, to the dry cleaners, and then to a drive through. When I got back from that trip, Sergeant Tiger made a beeline for me, reprimanded me, and threatened me with punishment of UCMJ (Uniform Code of Military Justice) to neither look at nor talk to this sergeant again. This was from my neighbor, one of the few people who talked to me like a normal human being. I expelled my breath, and my eyes welled with tears, hearing I was about to lose permission to talk to one of the three people who treated me kind and weren't trying to get in my pants. I was only trying to help, and I knew about the Army fraternization rule. In the Army, soldiers are not permitted to date people if they are in a position of authority over them, and I was a lower rank, a measly PFC (private first class).

Sergeant Tiger drew up a counseling statement.

"He's a sergeant, and you're a private."

"Okay, I'm not trying to date him. We are just friends," I defended.

"He's part of leadership, and this is fraternization! You are not to have any contact with him. If you even glance at him in the hallway, I'll write you up again for disobeying my orders. Besides, he isn't a good guy. Don't trust him. It's dangerous to even be friends with him," she warned.

I did not believe he was evil. One day, I peeked inside her open door and glimpsed artwork in Sergeant Tiger's room of herself wrapped in nothing but fur. The painting was crafted by none other than Sergeant Jay.

Looking back, I could maybe perceive some history between them—maybe a woman scorned? Maybe she cared about me and didn't want to take advantage of me? Later, I ended up paying Sergeant Jay to render a painting of my dad and me, and I never received my artwork or my money back. Maybe she knew more than she said. Figuring out what drives people was an adventure, as was discovering who I was in this unfamiliar world.

Chapter 3

Stalker

One particularly cloudy night, two months later, I decided I needed to drown my sorrows in some mint chocolate chip ice cream. It was 9 P.M., and the only place open on post was the one and only gas station. Days ago, after my sergeant announced she would no longer give me a ride to work, I had to get a car. There were no taxis or buses on post, and it was miles from our barracks to our chapel, with no connecting sidewalks to get there. I hastily bought myself a 2003 champagne-colored Dodge Neon, which I named Nina. I threw my bag on the passenger seat, wriggled to adjust my denim skirt, and hopped into my car. About half a mile down the road, I noticed a car that had also been at the gas station. I shrugged, we probably lived in the same place. There were three floors in my barracks, and I had been in Alaska a little over a month, so I didn't even know everyone in my unit.

I found a parking spot as the sky as the clouds rolled in, and wriggled my keys out of the ignition. My wallet fell, so I scooped it up and grabbed my bag, as someone knocked on the glass of my window. I yelled and jumped, and I hit my head on the roof of my car. The soldier who had startled me, laughed and flashed a smile, as I creaked the door slightly open. "Sorry, I didn't mean to startle you. What's your name?"

I felt embarrassed that I yelled. My voice quavered as I answered, "Um… Lorin."

"Didn't you see me trying to get your attention? I was flashing my lights at you and everything!" I thought I saw lights flashing, but it had started drizzling, and I assumed he had only turned his lights on and hit some bumps on the road.

"Um… no. Is there something wrong with my car? Do I have a light out?"

"No. I just saw you across the gas station store, and I had to know your name."

Wait… did he just say he followed me to my barracks, where I lived, to know my name? It was getting late. The sky was dark, and it started raining, but as I contemplated what to do, rain began to pour more rapidly from the sky. I spotted some soldiers outside my barracks in the smoking area.

Get to where there are people! "Okay. I gotta go," I told him.

"I'll walk with you," he insisted. It terrified me to try to figure out how to get rid of this guy and get into my room without him knowing where I lived. *You are an idiot*, I told myself. *Now he knows where you live! Hold on. There are three floors and plenty of rooms, so he doesn't know exactly where you live. Just don't go to your room, and don't let him know anything else about you.*

I walked faster, almost jogging as he tried to make small talk.

Stalker

I made it to the smokers quickly. I'm sure my short, stubby legs have never worked so fast in my life. He kept up with me, and as he recognized one smoker and started up a conversation, I thought I could sneak away, exit stage right.

"Wait! I didn't tell you my name. It's James," he shouted, as he bolted up beside me.

Uh oh… Think, Lorin. Think.

"You know, I'm not interested, and I really have to be going," I replied. He kept pressing me, inching closer. He wasn't taking no for an answer. "Listen," I said as smoothly as possible, "I already have a boyfriend, and he will not be okay with us talking, so I really need you to go now." He insisted he wasn't scared of my "boyfriend."

"Well, you are going to cause me a lot of grief, so please go." I was panicking by the stairs. I couldn't let him know where I lived. I had to think of something to scare him away.

"My boyfriend is six feet, three inches, he's ripped, and he's jealous. So, please just leave me alone!"

He gave me a look, and I was under the impression he wasn't going to stop, so I blurted out, "He's black too, so you know he doesn't play." James begrudgingly turned away.

I am ashamed that I spoke that last line. I assumed that because James was black, he would stop harassing me if he thought my boyfriend was black, but if he thought my "boyfriend" was white, he wouldn't have. In society, there is a problem where the mere presence of someone black, especially a guy, causes people to get intimidated and assume they are in danger. Black guys are labeled as aggressive. I feel ashamed as I write those lines down. It's the bias I have witnessed that makes a woman clutch her purse when she sees a black man, or crosses the street to avoid a black person, and it's a sad and common stereotype in our society.

To my relief, I watched James turn around and walk away. I waited until he was halfway to his car before I raced down the hall. My hands trembled as I unlocked the door. I missed the keyhole three times before I could align it and turn the knob. I closed the door as quickly as I could, as my heart felt as if it would jump out of my chest. I slid down the door to the floor, listening for any footsteps down the hall and praying to Jesus to help me. *Jesus, help me. Jesus, don't let him know where I live.*

The next day at formation, Sergeant Tiger asked me about my whereabouts the night before, saying, "I noticed you got in late." In reality, it was only about 9:30 P.M. *Here we go! She probably will think I am lying.*

I told Sergeant Tiger what had happened, so she at least knew about it if it were to happen again. Luckily for me, James had his uniform on, so I could identify him by his last name and unit patch. Her mouth gaped open, and she took a step back.

"Hey, I know that guy! We went to the leadership course together! Wait… he's married! That's weird. Why would he do that?"

"Sergeant, I don't know, but I am creeped out. What do I do, Sergeant?" I asked.

"I don't think he'll be bothering you again. Don't worry, but I guess just let me know if he does." And that was that. At the time, I thought that James never bothered me again because his ego was hurt, but maybe my sergeant had called him out. Maybe she stood in the gap for me. I may never know. Sergeant Tiger wasn't my favorite, but she wasn't all bad. She seemed to care, even if she had a funny way of showing it.

There were many instances of this harassment happening to other female soldiers. I guess there wasn't much accountability, and being in a force where most soldiers were men, most women are meant to feel as if they are the problem. They are made out to be too sensitive, too much to handle, and not enough, all at the same time. So women don't speak out, or when they do, they're silenced.

Eventually, I started dating and met a lot of pleasant guys who ended up not being my type, and some guys were downright creepy. One time, a thirty-five-year-old tried his best to win my affection.

"Um… I'm nineteen. My parents are maybe two years older than you. No."

I grew up in a conservative home where I had been lucky never to have had to encounter the real world. It may have been my parents' strict rules (which I am now grateful for), or just that I had yet to experience the amount of infidelity that couples experienced, married people included, in the Army, and it was shocking when I saw it. I was about to take a crash course.

Chapter 4

Caribbean Blues

Summer days in Alaska consisted of a bright beaming light streaming through your window until three or four in the morning. It was on one such day in July that I was not feeling so great, so I made my way to sick call. The Army lingo "sick call" simply means going to the medics for a sickness or injury. I was scared of my first sergeant and had been holding in my urine during PT (physical training) instead of using the restroom. He got really annoyed and started yelling and cursing. It was unnerving when it happened to others, so I would not stand out. I found it embarrassing to have to ask in front of other adults to use the latrine (bathroom). That cost me greatly because I wound up with my first urinary tract infection. In the Army, simple everyday actions, like using a bathroom, are micromanaged. Soldiers have to ask permission to do almost anything, due to the focus on accountability order, including getting a signed form to hand in to sick call. I told Sergeant Tiger on Friday because I was in pain. I never had a UTI (urinary tract infection) personally, but I was aware of the symptoms. So, Sergeant

Caribbean Blues

Tiger ordered me to carry around cranberry juice through the weekend and gulp from it every five minutes. She easily monitored me as we worked chapel duty on Sunday and were tasked out to help at a function off post as well. I longed for the weekend to be over. Sick call hours were Monday through Friday, from 5:30 A.M. until 7 A.M., so I had to wait until Monday to get myself checked out.

Upon arriving at sick call, I waited for my turn for the medic to take my vitals and ask pre-screening questions. The medical staff ushered me into one of the patient rooms. The medic, Cypress, was pleasant. He was charming and had a wonderful island accent that I found striking.

"You sound familiar to me. Where are you from?" he asked.

"I'm from New York," I replied.

"What part? I'm from the Bronx. Well, I am from the Caribbean, but I moved to New York. Okay, let me ask you a few questions. What brings you here today?

I could feel my face flush, "Um… I think I have a urinary tract infection," I nervously replied.

I had to tell him my symptoms, and I had known someone in my family who was prone to them, so I knew the symptoms, though this was my first time experiencing one.

"Just how do you think you got it?" he questioned.

I stared at the floor.

"Um… from holding in my urine. I'm new, and I didn't want to tell my first sergeant."

My ears felt hot. He chuckled.

"That would do it."

After the nurse practitioner came and went, he knocked and slipped back in the door, talking to me some more. He talked to me about my medicine and gave me instructions. Then he slipped me his number on a piece of paper.

"Call me, so we can go out sometime. I know how New York girls are—you don't like giving out your numbers, but I enjoy talking with you and would like to talk to you some more."

I waited the obligatory few days before I called. You know, those are the unspoken rules of trying not to seem clingy or too desperate? Then we went out on a few dates. He was funny, but he asked if I was crazy because, "New York women are crazy!" I have been told I have an old soul, so I liked that Cypress was twenty-seven. We talked about our faith, and it made me happy to have met a man with the same beliefs. Cypress told me he wanted to settle down, and my heart fluttered when he told me how I would be good wife, and he couldn't wait for me to have his kids. As a nineteen-year-old, I was already over dating for fun. I wanted to date someone who I felt at least had the potential to be marriage material. I had decided I would be married by twenty-one and be done with my college classes by twenty-four. This was exactly the kind of relationship I wanted. I mused, *This is why you should date older guys.* Cypress always knew how to make me feel good about myself. He showered me with compliments, calling me beautiful, sexy, and smart. He never opened car doors for me, because he said, "We are equal, and I know women in New York want to be treated as equals." He cracked me up with his jokes and his quick smirk. He was ambitious, a hard worker, just like my dad, and his accent melted me into a puddle. Cypress was going to school full time while in the Army and was making future plans with me. After a few months of dating, after we had gone to the movies and he was dropping me off at my barracks, I thought it was about time I should meet his friends. I felt nervous for the answer after asking him about it. Maybe he didn't think his friends would like me.

"Why haven't I met your friends? Do some of your friends live in your barracks?" I asked him.

"They are busy, and I am always at work or school."

"It would only be like for ten minutes, unless you are hiding me because you don't think they will like me. Are you ashamed of me? Is it because I'm only nineteen? What is going on?" I pressed.

"See? You New York women are crazy. There is nothing going on. You acting crazy!" He chuckled at me.

Finally, I nagged him so much that he gave in and set up a time for me to meet his friends. It was at a local favorite restaurant. His four guy friends and one female friend were seated at the bar. They all stared at me. I felt their eyes scanning me. They said hello to me, but something was off. They were aloof. The female friend crossed her arms and narrowed her eyes at me. I chalked it up to me being the only white person in the group. The other guys said hello, but they, too, were standoffish. I tried to engage in conversation.

"So, how long have you guys been in Alaska?"

One didn't bother to answer, and the other three answered me with as few words as possible. I tried again.

"I'm from New York. Where are you guys from?"

Some of them muttered back one word answers. After about fifteen minutes, Cypress said we had to go, so I left with him. I was puzzled.

"So, that was weird right? I don't think that went well at all. I think your friends hate me. Did I do something wrong?" I inquired.

"Nah. They just need to get to know you more. They are protective of me because they are my friends, and they don't know you yet. Once they get to know you, I'm sure they will love you like I do," he reassured.

"Wait… you love me? Wow! I think I might love you too!" I exclaimed.

"Yes. I said I want you to have my kids. I want to take you to meet my mom on our island. I am going to marry you."

I blushed. "I just thought you were being sweet or joking."

I never asked to hang with his friends again. We went out to restaurants and movies, and he visited me at my barracks. I reasoned that maybe he didn't want me to meet his friends because he knew they wouldn't like me. Maybe they didn't like me because I was white. But… never mind that. My boyfriend told me he loved me, and he wanted to marry me. I was so certain that he may pop the question any day, officially with a ring.

We continued dating, and things progressed into a more intimate relationship. I reasoned away my guilt from my Christian upbringing. He loved me, and he was going to marry me. He started calling me "wifey," and I was thinking, This is what it takes in a grown relationship. He loves me, and he wants me. We are going to be married anyway. I started to see him only once a week, and he always wanted to stay in. I started to feel weird. I questioned if he still was ashamed of me. Sometimes, I met him at his barracks parking lot, and we drove somewhere, so we could go on our dates, but we had our own cars to go our separate ways at the end. Maybe it was because he was so busy that he was tired and didn't want to go out. I pushed my thoughts of doubt out of my head. I worry too much.

We talked on the phone most every day. After a few months of seeing him maybe only four times during the month, I decided to drive to his barracks because he told me he was studying in his room for his college class, which was why he couldn't see me. I had to see him! That's weird. His car isn't in the parking lot. I texted him, as my stomach twisted up in knots.

I texted him. "Hey. I was in the area near the barracks and wanted to stop by. Why aren't you here?"

He texted me back. "You're jealous and crazy. You spying on me? Lol."

"No. I wanted to see you, and you said you were going to be studying at home. So where are you?"

"I was studying, but I got hungry and went with my friends to eat. I'm downtown, eating on Main Street. We are leaving soon. I have to get back to studying. Talk to you later."

I felt a knot in my stomach. Why didn't he ask me to bring him food or ask me to go out with him? If it was the same friends as last time, I didn't want it to be awkward again. I called Kay.

"Hey. Do you want to come with me? I want to go see if I can find Cypress. He is eating downtown somewhere, and I don't want to go alone."

"What restaurant?" she asked.

"I don't know. But it feels weird, so I just feel I need to go."

"Sure." When I knocked on her barracks door, she came out, her forehead wrinkled.

"You okay?"

I bit my lip and nodded. We got into my car, and I headed to downtown Fairbanks. There were only a handful of restaurants he could be in. As I stalked up and down the streets, I squinted my eyes and locked my jaw. It would be easy to spot his car, with the Caribbean flag dangling from the rearview mirror. I drove around the same few blocks a couple of times.

I couldn't see his car, so I called him.

He didn't answer at first. After the fourth time going to voicemail, he texted me.

"Sorry. My phone died," he explained.

"Where were you?" I demanded.

"I told you. I was eating with my friends and then I stopped at the store for a few things, and now I'm at the library."

I called him, and he picked up.

"I went downtown, and I didn't see you anywhere. Where are you, really? Who are you with?" I questioned.

Caribbean Blues

"I was downtown, Woman," he defended.

"I didn't see your car."

"You stalking me?" He laughed. "New York women are crazy. You acting crazy and jealous. I don't know why you didn't see my car, but I was there. I am sorry I haven't seen you lately, but with work and school, I've been too busy. You acting crazy, though. Calm down."

Maybe I overlooked his car, I thought. I swore I barely went four mph through those streets, scanning for his car, but I was pretty upset. I could have overlooked it, and I didn't want to be that jealous girlfriend. Maybe he was right. I never have caught him doing anything wrong. Still, something wasn't right.

A few months later, we were planning to go on a date, but he called me to cancel our date because he had smallpox and claimed it was contagious. I hung up the phone.

Wait. People don't get smallpox anymore! I am an idiot. So, I grabbed my car keys and flew to his barracks, sure that I would catch him in his lie. Every barracks has a CQ desk (Charge of Quarters) where they checked visitor's identification, and visitors had to know the room number in order to fill out the sign-in sheet.

The barracks are like dorm rooms that college students use. The CQ desk soldier's job was to make sure the guests visiting were eighteen years of age or older and that there was no "funny business" happening. Underage guests were an enormous problem. Many of the soldiers in the infantry got caught bringing young female guests home. A lot of infantrymen were in the eighteen to twenty-five year range, and some guys got caught taking home girls that were maybe fifteen or sixteen.

I finagled my way to getting them to give me his room number. I told them I forgot the number and acted as if I had just been there a few days ago. I spotted Cypress in the middle of the hallway and approached him like a stealthy ninja.

Cypress took two steps back, and his eyes bulged as I reached him.

"What are you doing here?" he asked.

"Smallpox?!? No one gets smallpox anymore. That's why we have vaccinations for it!" I hissed at him.

He started pointing to his arm.

"Look, woman, this is what I'm talking about." He pointed to his bandaged arm and chuckled.

"You can get smallpox if our arms touch, so that's why I stayed away. Come here. You New York women are so crazy! I had to get this shot before deployment."

He invited me into his barracks room. I scanned the room for any sign of suspicious activity. We talked about his deployment.

"A year is a long time, and we have only been dating for a few months. Did you want to take a break?" he asked.

"Do you still love me? Do you still want to marry me?"

"Of course I do. Why are you so crazy?"

"Then, if you do, we should stay together," I said.

Nearly a week later, I was cleaning my room and dancing around when my phone rang. I saw my roommate Danica's number pop up, so

Caribbean Blues

I answered it.

"Hey, Lorin. I am a 'plus one' for a friend at a backyard wedding. I'm just checking, but I need to know if you are still dating Cypress?"

"Yes. Why? What's wrong? Is he with another date at the wedding?" I knew he was cheating on me!

"No Lorin. You don't understand. I don't know how to tell you this, so I am just going to say it. I am at his wedding!"

All my blood drained from my face. My legs felt weak. I needed to sit down. I blinked rapidly, as I froze in front of our couch. I felt as though I was sucker-punched.

"What do you mean? Are you sure?"

"I am standing maybe twenty feet away, and I just watched them exchange vows and everything," she explained.

"Wait. Who is she? Do I know her?"

"I don't think so. I know her though. She was in my arctic training course. It's kind of weird because she looks a little like you as far as size and hair, but you are way prettier. I am so sorry! I didn't even know this was his wedding! Are you going to be okay? I am so sorry! Lorin, are you there? Are you okay?"

I swallowed the lump in my throat. "Um… yes, I mean, I think so."

Feeling shaky, I hung up the phone. My legs were unable to carry the weight, so I stepped backward and bent my knees as I pushed my back into the cushion of our uncomfortable green sofa. My stomach twisted. I sat there for thirty minutes, shaking my head, as I tried to process what I had just learned. The man I thought I would marry, who I thought I loved and that he loved me, married another woman.

Danica's words echoed in my head. "I'm at his wedding." Heat rushed through my entire body at that moment. My body stiffened as I balled my fists. That was supposed to be my ceremony, my friends, my vows, my husband! My mind raced and linked up with all the oddities that have endured the course of our relationship, such as the friends acting weird when they met me. It was because there was someone else. It all made sense now. The scarcity of time together wasn't because he was training for deployment. It wasn't because he was in those college classes. There was someone else, another woman he had to spend time with. The reason he called me "sexy" or "wifey" was because he was with someone else. He called me "sexy," so he didn't mess up and call me by the wrong name. The reason we didn't go to his barracks was because she lived there too. She was in the medical unit. The reason my gut told me something was going on was because there actually was something going on. He was cheating on me! And then the realization hit me. It was as if an elephant had plopped itself right on my chest. He wasn't cheating on me—he was cheating with me!

Hot tears streamed down my face. For about another hour, I contemplated what I would do. I didn't know what to think, but I knew I wanted to tell him off. I called his phone, and it went to voicemail. I hung up. I imagined Cypress and his cute blonde wife dancing, cutting the cake, laughing, and I felt my blood boil. I felt I was going to crush the phone I had pressed so tightly to my chest.

So, I called him again. As the phone rang, my heart was beating out of my chest, and I could feel a sharp throbbing pain rising up, as a lump in my throat formed. His voice echoed in my ear to leave a message. Oh, did I ever!

I started off in a chipper voice, "I am hurt that I didn't get an invitation to your wedding." My voice got louder, "My invitation must have got lost in the mail."

Then I exploded. I yelled at my phone. I called him every curse word I could think of. I'm not even sure I did it right or used them right. Growing up in a Christian environment, cursing wasn't allowed in my house, but it felt good in the moment to just rattle off a few explicit words and phrases I knew my mom would not be proud of.

"You lying scumbag. You fatherless child. You are a trucking jerk, a female dog!"

As the poisonous words escaped my mouth, my ears pounded, as I screamed how he was the worst human being on the face of the planet!

After he returned from his honeymoon, he called me back, and I answered. I don't know what I expected him to say, but all he could muster was some ridiculous excuse about how this was an ex-girlfriend he knew prior to me. Cypress explained he got married on a whim because he needed the extra money to give his family to move from the islands to the states.

"If that is true, why wouldn't you have married me? You are a liar. Why are you calling me? Don't you have a wife to attend to?" He told me he forgot his dog tags at my barracks.

"Not my problem."

"But I am deploying soon, and I need them," he reasoned.

Fine… I needed him out of my life and not to be getting me into any trouble. This way, he had to look me in my eye, I thought. He had the nerve to show up at my barracks the next night to ask for these doggone tags and smile at me.

"Aren't you going to invite me in?"

"Why are you here at these barracks? Clearly you have a wedding ring and are a married man. Why would a married man come to where single people live?"

"Shh… shush. Okay. Okay. You're gonna get me into trouble. You're mad at me, but if you would let me explain…"

"What is there to explain? What you need to explain to everyone is why a married man is here trying to talk to me!"

I punched him in his chest, once, twice, and again for good measure.

"Ow! Okay, okay. Do you feel better? Am I going to have to worry about you slashing my tires?"

Really? You want to poke the bear? He asked again for his dog tags.

"Oh, these? Here. Go get them!" I tossed them off the stairs in the front of our building and pushed him. "Don't ever, ever come near me again! Don't speak to me! You are dead to me," something dramatic I must have picked up from my Italian side or, possibly, The Godfather.

I stormed back into my room and slammed the door. There was no way I was going to let him see me cry. It was then that I felt my heart sink, and I couldn't breathe. My heart felt as if someone had taken it out of my body and stomped on it. I covered my tear stricken face with my hands. My eyes were swollen and red, stinging with the flow of my salty tears. I mourned the death of my future, of love, and of a connection that wasn't real.

Life's biggest teacher is experience. I learned how to tell a tree by its fruit. It was my first personal experience that religion doesn't make a person good. It wasn't the first time I doubted myself, but it was the first time I saw that not everyone was for me, even if they claimed to be. I had the choice to listen to that small, still voice or ignore it.

After my real life soap opera played out before me, I swore off dating forever. I was destined to live alone in a dilapidated shack, with myself and twenty cats. I wasn't even a fan of cats! I felt so stupid. Why didn't I listen to my gut? Why didn't I just end it one of those times I felt it was off?

After our break up, I went to work, finished my tasks each day, and went home. This was my life now. I buried myself in my college classes and at work, helping other people's hurts, so I didn't have to deal with my own. I ran the chapel programs and worked two positions above my own. Within a matter of months, my heart changed with the weather. I had gone from warm and airy to cool and crisp, as summer turned into fall.

Chapter 5

Seasons Change

Time went on, and suddenly I could breathe deeply again. I inhaled the October breeze. It had already snowed a few times because, in Alaska, winter weather started at the end of September and typically ended mid-April. Both of my sergeants left to go on to their next duty stations, and the chaplains had gone ahead to either deployments or their next assignments. It was just me with one other chaplain assistant, Specialist Fox. Fox was four years older than me and a character. He ran the other chapel and had a reputation for being able to wriggle out of work. Fox delegated most of his job to other soldiers who were on extra duty for getting into trouble. He managed to "wheel and deal" his way out of work so effortlessly. Looking back, I would say that he was resourceful, such as the time he had all the chapel calls forwarded to his cell phone because he lived five minutes away and would rather be at home.

Specialist Fox pulled me aside after our Monday morning chaplain meeting. "Sergeant Tiger gave me this folder to give to our next sergeant," he said, as though this should mean something to me. I raised my eyebrow.

"Okay? Why are you telling me?"

"It was full of our counseling," he explained. "But, don't worry. I got rid of all the negative ones that had stupid reasons."

I opened my mouth to argue. Maybe he shouldn't have done that, but I closed my mouth almost immediately. A clean slate with our next sergeant wouldn't be so bad, I reasoned.

As if he was reading my mind, Fox said, "I can't believe some of the counseling statements she did for you."

I nodded in agreement. A counseling statement is a quarterly review of how well you did your job. Your supervisor could call a meeting and give you a counseling statement for excellent or poor job performance. If you never had an initial counseling statement, there was no documentation of expectations. A supervisor could invent new rules or expectations as they deemed necessary.. Non-Commissioned Officer Evaluation Reviews (NCOERs) followed sergeants throughout their career, but weren't used for soldiers that were lower ranking. These evaluations were more formal and important to an Army career. The quarterly reviews could afford justifications for promotions or keep soldiers from being promoted. Every time they put a new supervisor in charge, even if there was a hand off of responsibilities, a soldier could start with a clean slate. When Sergeant Tiger left, she handed them off to Fox, so they'd still be on the record, and boy were there some dumb ones in there!

The whole reason I had gotten my Neon back in June was

Seasons Change

because of the counseling statement I received for borrowing another chaplain assistant's car. I had my driver license but no car and a responsibility to get myself to work. There were no sidewalks or public transportation at Fort Wainwright. Feeling like a taxi and having to ride with her subordinate, Sergeant Tiger was tired of helping me get around, and I had to figure out my ride situation. She told me I needed to find transportation to work on my own. Fair enough. I talked to a fellow chaplain, Assistant Specialist Spark, about borrowing his car while he was away for two months of training, while I looked for a car.

I let her know that I found a solution.

"Why would he let you borrow his car? He doesn't know you. You can't drive his car for that amount of time. What if something happens when you are driving his car? You can't if you don't have insurance," she said with her arms crossed across her chest.

I checked with Specialist Spark, and he said his insurance covered me borrowing his car, so I didn't have to get my own.

Thinking she would stop pestering me, I told Sergeant Tiger. Instead, her jaw clenched, her eyes flashed, and her nostrils flared.

"I forbid you to drive that car! You cannot drive someone else's car and not have your own insurance!"

"Sergeant, you told me I had to find a way, and I did. Specialist Spark checked with his insurance, and it was okay!" I protested.

"If you disobey again, I will write you up for insubordination. In fact, come to my office now. We are going to sign a counseling statement."

Another time, I got a counseling statement for getting a sunburn. I went tanning in a tanning booth with my friend, who was of Mexican descent. I asked her how long to tan for, as she was doing fifteen minutes.

"Don't put on sunscreen. Just do two minutes," she instructed me.

When I emerged from the tanning booth, I was fire-engine red. No aloe vera balm could heal my skin fast enough, and since it was a standing booth, I was burnt everywhere. When I say everywhere, I mean everywhere. I couldn't sit, walk, or put my hands down without wincing in pain. That Monday, I went into the chapel, and Sergeant Tiger caught a glimpse of me.

"Whiteman, come in here!" She gestured wildly at me, "What is this that I see?"

"Sergeant?"

"What is wrong with this picture? What is all this redness all over you?"

I was confused and thought she was joking with me.

"Just a sunburn, Sergeant."

"Wipe that smirk off your face! It's not just a sunburn. It's destruction of government property. A sunburn is a hindrance to your ability to work. A sunburn causes yourself injury. The Army owns you. I'm writing you up. Next time, it will be an Article 15."

Specialist Fox and I held down the fort, supporting the 172nd infantry, being tasked out for many things that were neither in our job description nor something we should have had to do, but as the months

Seasons Change

went on, our company grew smaller and smaller. All the soldiers, including firefighters and air traffic control, had to re-class (change their job or get out of our garrison unit). I was getting settled in at my job. I worked two areas of operation: the Family Life Counseling Center and the Chapel, as well as taking care of the official mail for the chaplain's office. We were being tasked out for "details" (extra manual labor or jobs unrelated to our occupations). As chaplain assistants, we needed to be exempt for many of these extra tasks, including CQ duty, (Charge of Quarter, or security for who passes in and out of the barracks). As chaplain assistants, we were on standby to be called into work or duty by our chaplains. The on-call chaplain was rotating between chaplains for emergency instances—suicides—the painful scene that is more real than how the movies portrayed it. There were also the support visits to the spouses and families of those who didn't make it back from deployment, as well as hospital visits for giving last rites. Chaplain assistants already had a built-in extra duty where we rotated at the chapel on Saturdays and Sundays for religious services, as well as other days to open and run the chapel for events outside of the normal operating hours.

During our weekly meeting for the chaplain section, we found out we were receiving an incoming NCO (noncommissioned officer), our new supervisor, at the end of the month.

Sergeant Church was a slim, white male who wore faded jeans with ripped knees and had tattoos that danced up and down his forearms. He was a recently promoted sergeant, and he had yet to go to the leadership course, which was the training school a sergeant had to attend within a year of promotion. Sergeant Church seemed a little goofy, but he was nice enough.

One day, as we were driving in the chaplain office government work truck, he told me we were receiving another soldier. We were both excited because there was a lot of work put on his and my shoulders (because Specialist Fox always finagled his way out of duties), and everyone had been working with few or no breaks because we were short staffed. The 172nd Infantry Division had deployed, so we worked every weekend with no relief. I seemed to get a lot of the extra duties because they all knew I was responsible. When Specialist Fox went off to different training schools, I was in charge of three areas of operation: both of the chapels and the Chaplain Family Life Center. I also was responsible for the hospital chapel, incomers' briefings, picking up the official mail, and various random things.

"Now, PFC Whiteman, this soldier has just been through a divorce and is vulnerable, so please let him be," Sergeant Church warned me.

"What do you mean, Sergeant? I am not a mean person."

He raised his eyebrow and tilted his head to the side. "I know. I also know you love black guys, and I need you to leave him alone."

I had dated a few times in high school, and they happened to be white. However, since being on the dating scene in Alaska, he knew I had dated some Hispanic and black guys in the past months. I have always appreciated darker skin than mine, but that includes everyone else because my skin is usually the palest shade. My mom liked to tell the story of me when I was four, growing up in Brooklyn. As a child, I was petite, with blue eyes and long, blonde hair. We walked past a bunch of construction workers, when I yelled, "Mommy! Look at the black man!"

"Uh huh… come on," my mom said, as her cheeks flushed pink.

"But mom! Look at the black man!" I was in awe. The construction crew laughed. My mom was trying to usher me along,

Seasons Change

"Uh… yes, I see. Now, let's go."

I had never appreciated my pale skin. I tend to turn bright red in the sun, and my legs are as white as Casper. Even though my maternal grandmothers were Italian on both parents' sides, I inherited none of that blessed olive, glowing skin that some of my cousins had. My skin displayed my Northern European roots, from both of my grandfathers of Irish, German, French, and English descent.

It's true that I had dated black guys, but they were guys who just happened to be black. I wasn't intentionally searching for a love interest based on skin color. I tried my best not to let him see me roll my eyes.

"Sergeant, just because he's black doesn't mean I will date him," I defended.

I was indignant. I couldn't care less, and I was going to prove that to Sergeant Church.

Chapter 6

First Impressions to Lasting Impact

Lord knows it was too early in the morning to be awake, and the dark and cold month of November was here. I slapped my alarm clock one too many times. On the last snooze, I heard my clock's glaring siren and turned to see it blinking a red 6:15 A.M. Uh-oh! I rolled out of bed, brushed my teeth, threw on my clothes for PT, and threw my hair up into the obligatory bun, and I wiped the sleep from my eyes. It was a good thing formation was in the same building! I ran down the stairs to where our formation met every morning during the winter. Formation was at 6:30 A.M. sharp, but they expected me to be there before that time. I arrived five minutes later than I should have. In the Army, if you're not early, you're late. The rule was we were to arrive fifteen minutes before an event. The other soldiers in my unit glanced my way. I was lucky my boss wasn't there yet. I was born late, in fact, two days late. I have always felt that has been a constant theme of my life. I am always rushing around at

First Impressions to Lasting Impact

the last minute, scrambling through the door.

Sergeant Church walked into the basement area. During the morning formation, with all of us standing at parade rest, the company welcomed Specialist Stephen Hayes. I was curious but tired, so I didn't really look at him until our platoon leader called for us to fall out.

We broke formation and were released to get ready for our duties for the day.

Sergeant Church approached, the new guy in tow, and stepped to the side. "Whiteman, I want you to meet Specialist Hayes. He is our new chaplain assistant."

"Nice to meet you," I said to him. He flashed an infectious smile, and I was a little startled because he was cute. He had kind, dark brown eyes, a freshly faded haircut, and creamy mocha java cocoa skin (his words). I smiled back and felt my cheeks grow warm. "Hi. Welcome to Alaska."

We went opposite ways to prepare for the day.

Later that evening, after I had just gotten off of work, I was hungry. I needed to get some food, and Specialist Hayes flashed in my mind. I remembered how it was lonely and hard for me at first. His car wouldn't ship for two months because Alaska is far away, and, I admit, I wondered what the handsome Specialist Hayes was doing. I imagined him sitting in his room. Was he watching TV? Then I realized he wouldn't have any of his stuff yet because the Army takes a few months to ship household goods, so he wouldn't have a TV yet. What sports did he like? Was he reading a novel? Maybe he was listening to music. Did he like the same music I did? What if he was lonely and homesick?

I let my hair down out of my neatly Army-approved bun, ran a flat iron through my tresses, threw on my favorite dark wash jeans and a long-sleeved tee, and donned my royal blue puffer jacket. I applied lip balm and reapplied some mascara in the mirror. I caught my reflection in the mirror and told myself I was just being friendly to someone who was new and doesn't know anyone, right? I grabbed my car keys. Slowly, I made my way down the hallway toward his room. I almost chickened out and turned away, but I pivoted back and knocked on his barracks door, rubbing my hand on my arm. He opened the door, surprised.

"Hello," he said.

"Hey. So, I know how it was when I first got here, and I wanted to let you know that if you have questions or something, I can help." My stomach grumbled, and I blushed. "So, I was going to grab a bite to eat. Would you want to come?"

"Yes! Yes, please! Sergeant Church was supposed to take me to the store, so I could have a few groceries for this mini-fridge, but then he didn't want to go anymore because he forgot and had already gone without me. I was just trying to figure out how I was going to eat."

The Army base was too big to walk around, and the only food places besides the DFAC (dining facility), which was across the base, was outside the post. There was no public transportation, and it was a frigid negative ten degrees. Every place is five miles away, with no sidewalks to get there.

I am typically not a fan of daily driving. I would rather have someone else sit in the driver seat while I tag along in the passenger seat. Driving causes me anxiety, more so in the snow.

"Would you be willing to drive my car?"

He looked puzzled but shrugged and nodded. I tossed him my keys, and he opened the passenger door for me and hopped into the driver's seat.

First Impressions to Lasting Impact

"Let's play twenty questions!" I glanced at him.

"What, am I on trial here?" He smirked.

"No, but I don't know too much about you besides what Sergeant Church said. So, what made you pick Alaska?"

"I didn't. My ex did. What did you hear about me—that I was charming and debonair?"

He raised his eyebrows a few times and let out a loud laugh, the kind of laugh that makes you want to laugh and be in on the joke.

My face turned pink.

"Um… that you were newly divorced. Oh, I'm sorry. You probably don't want to talk about that. Well, I hope Alaska grows on you. I didn't really want to be here either, but you may be surprised. Sometimes people make it bearable. Turn here. So, where are you from?" I wanted to hear about him, not have to awkwardly answer.

"Texas. Well, I call Texas home because my mom was in the Navy, and I spent most my life there with her and my sister."

"Are you close with your family?"

"Yes. I grew up with my younger sister, Brenita, and I later found out my dad had two other daughters, so I have three sisters. I am close with my family. How about you?"

He glanced at me a few times, smiling as he waited for my answer. He made me feel as though he was interested in what I had to say. He wanted to know me!

"I'm from New York. I grew up with a sister, too. She's almost six years younger than me. Then, my uncle, who is actually my age, came to live with us when my dad's mom died, so I kinda have a brother, too."

I decided to be nosy.

"So, you don't have to answer this, but why did you get divorced."

"She found someone else."

"Ouch. I'm sorry."

"Yep. My family keeps telling me that I might find myself an Alaskan to marry. Not that I'm looking, but I think they are trying to make me feel better."

"Hmm… I'm afraid the ratio is in favor of women here. It's something like one woman to every eight men."

His eyes twinkled, and his dimples flashed. "So, I am lucky to be in your presence then?"

I laughed, but I felt that he really meant what he said.

Something was different about him, different than other guys I dated. He was going places. He spoke about being a man of faith and that faith bringing him through one of his hardest seasons. We talked more, and the more I heard, the more I felt that this guy was special. I felt in my spirit that he had a good heart, and I was going to like getting to know him more. Even thought I knew Sergeant Church had warned me to leave him alone, I had not counted on me actually liking Hayes and wanting to be more than just friends.

Over time, I observed his knack for getting others engaged. He told animated stories and had the most infectious laugh. Using hand motions, he revealed stories of his experiences and stories of his youth, like how he and his friends used to "Frankenstein" bikes together. Hayes would not volunteer to test run them unless he had given the bike the once-over to make sure they tightened all the bolts. He talked about going downhill, as parts of the bike flew off and brakes failed, and they sailed through the air and crash landed. He confided in me his trust issues and told parts of some tough stories, but he still made parts of his stories lighter when he interjected a perfectly timed joke. He had a well-planned retort for everything, a playful grin, and a booming laugh. He held joy in his heart and kept his chin up, despite the circumstances that brought him to Alaska. He was confident. He knew who he was and whose he was. He was a child of God. He was loved and chosen. I needed to believe that more myself, too. I also wanted to feel that confidence that radiated from the inside.

Hayes was the epitome of a southern gentleman. He opened every single door for me. It sometimes annoyed me and my self-proclaimed feminist tendencies to not need a man's help, especially to wait in negative-forty-degree weather, to wait for Stephen to come around the car to open the door. He carried himself with an air of peace and strength. He could draw anyone in with his warmth and his welcoming spirit. He cared when others spoke. He leaned in when I shared stories or shared how I was feeling. He was easy to be around. And he was around, unlike my previous relationship. He was not dodgy. He engaged with me. I didn't have to chase him. He wanted to spend time with me.

I invited Hayes to every place and every activity, and we quickly became close friends, but I liked him more than just a friend. I liked him. I liked him a *lot*. As crazy as it sounds, I thought he could be the one, my forever love. Only, I wasn't sure if he felt the same or if he was ready for romantic ties. We had only known each other for a few weeks, and he and I both had gone through painful breakups.

One night, I invited him to watch a movie with me, but the entire time, I kept stealing glances at him and wondering if he liked me too. I scooted closer to him. He felt me staring at him. I blushed and tried to pretend I wasn't.

"What? What is it?"

My face flushed once again, and my heart drummed in my chest, "Um… it's nothing…"

However, he wasn't fooled, and he turned to face me, studying me closely. "No. I can tell it's something. What is it?"

Am I doing this? I thought, feeling that my palms were sweaty. Hayes was my friend. Who knew if he was into me or if he was dating. I didn't want to risk losing that friendship, but if he felt the same way I did… *Yeah. I'm doing this.* "Um," I stammered, steadying myself for the potential reaction, "I was just wondering if your lips were as soft as they looked because I want to kiss them." The words escaped my mouth and surprised me. I was never that forward. I glanced away, as my face felt hot and looked back at him, terrified when I couldn't read his expression.

But then he smiled. "Why don't you see for yourself?"

And that was it. I let my guard down. As we kissed, I felt all prickly on the back of my neck, and my heart felt as though it might leap through my chest.

Chapter 7
Chapel Duty & Extra Duty

Being a chaplain assistant is like being a Jack of all trades. In school, I had learned different religions recognized by the Army, as well as the accommodations soldiers were allotted as they served in the military. A chaplain had to have a Master of Divinity and have endorsement from their faith group. There are Muslim, Christian, Catholic, Jewish, and Buddhist chaplains I knew, but the chapel was a center any religious group could use. Sometimes Wiccans needed a spot to meet, or Jedi (not kidding about that being a religion) needed to practice their religion. Chaplain assistants learned about the different sacraments, about setting up a service, about liturgical colors in the chapel. We learned how to peer counsel soldiers. We were told that, as a Unit Ministry Team, our job was to check on the morale and welfare of the unit and make sure people were getting their needs meet. For example, there may be a Muslim soldier who needed accommodations because he was fasting. Part of our job was to make sure that people were receiving their religious accommodations. They taught us how to document and secure a chapel tithe and offering. They shared the seriousness of handling chapel money. If the money count was off, the responsible chaplain assistant could be accused of stealing money, which is a federal offense. The chaplain schoolhouse staff taught us tactical movements to protect the chaplain. They taught us how to give religious briefings at the commander's brief to make sure that everyone knew the holy days and religion of a region they deployed us to, in order to respect the culture and not offend the citizens. The instructors retrained us at the range to shoot our M-16s, and we learned about sidearms. They taught us to help organize prayer breakfasts and how to support the units we were attached to, as well as setting up for memorial services.

What I never recalled from the chaplain schoolhouse was being taught to maintain lawn equipment or snow blowers, or to order supplies from the two different sources of federal money, or many of the administration and management that were crucial for garrison assignments. A lot of the jobs for chaplain assistants were learned on-site. Typically, this is because every chapel is a little different, and every chaplain is different.

We helped with deployment briefings, suicide prevention training, Family Readiness Group for soldiers deploying, memorial services, vow renewals, Protestant chapel events, bible studies, and Catholic congregation events. We coordinated repairs, scheduled appointments, coordinated counseling for family and soldiers, offered peer counseling, referred soldiers, ordered supplies, completed administrative duties, planned and provided coverage for programs and events extending beyond normal duty hours.

Chapel Duty & Extra Duty

When Stephen first arrived to Fort Wainwright, we did on-the-job training, what the Army calls "left seat, right seat," to bring soldiers up to speed on what particularities a duty station had. After Stephen observed that all the expectations were on my shoulders, he started taking chances. He had groups help clean up after themselves, instead of leaving a mess for me to clean up after and having to disassemble and rearrange furniture after every event. A lot of parishioners did not like the changes he set in place. This alleviated stress, and while I still had to maintain the chapel and regular cleaning, the people who used the chapel had to clean up after themselves, and some were not used to having to do this, as their spouses or family members were higher ranking. This was evident one day, when a situation unfolded.

A chaplain's nine-year-old daughter spilled Kool-Aid on the floor in the foyer outside of the fellowship hall after Sunday service. She was supposed to keep the food in the fellowship hall, but she found Stephen who was busy with another task.

"There's a mess. I spilled a drink." She giggled and looked him in the face and tilted her head. "You are going to have to clean it up."

He squinted at her and said evenly, "No. I can't right now, but you can clean up the mess since you spilled it."

"Um... do you know who my daddy is?" Her dad was an officer who was much higher ranking than us, a full bird colonel, meaning he'd served at least nineteen years.

"No I don't, but it doesn't matter. I am in charge of this chapel, and I am not your maid."

He stepped around her to the broom closet and offered her the mop. She snatched the mop and grumbled, but she went to work and cleaned up the mess she made. He stood watch, and when she finished, he reached his arms out to take back the mop.

"Thank you for cleaning your mess."

As the unit dwindled down to just chaplain and chaplain assistant, we were tasked out for "special assignments"— chopping down brush and thick trees with nothing more than our entrenching tools, as well as weeding and backbreaking work, because the area near the airfield looked unkempt, and we were going to have a three-star general visit. We also had to do things like the distribution of official mail, personal mail, CQ duty, stuff we were supposed to be exempt from, as we already had extra duties for services every Sunday. We also had things after hours, such as bible study, praise team rehearsal, and whatever other extra group activity that used the chapel for meetings. However, we were still being tasked out for details (extra manual labor or jobs unrelated to my occupation). As chaplain assistants, we needed to be exempt for many of these extra tasks, as we were on standby to be called into work and duty by our chaplains. The on-call chaplain phone was rotated between chaplains for emergency instances, deaths, mental health crises, hospital visits, reciting last rites for soldiers who were dying, and notifying the next of kin when soldiers were killed in action. Chaplain assistants already had a built-in extra duty where we rotated at the chapel on Saturdays and Sundays for religious services and other days after work to open and run the chapel for events that occurred outside of normal operating hours.

More chaplain assistants arrived, which was a relief. Sergeant Waters worked at the other chapel, and we started to get to know him better at all the mandatory teambuilding functions. He played on the unit softball team with us as well. Sergeant Waters and his wife had two daughters. After one of the teambuilding events, he pulled me aside.

"Hey. What are you doing this Friday? Do you think you could watch my kids, so me and the wife can go out? I can even pay you. It will be easy.

They will just be in their rooms because it will be past their bedtimes, so you could just watch a movie or something downstairs."

"I can help, but you don't have to pay me this time."

I had grown up babysitting for others at my church and helping in the kid's ministry, so it was no problem for me. This would be the perfect time to see how Stephen was around kids, since I knew I eventually wanted three or four kids.

I pleaded with my eyes. "Stephen, will you please come with me to Sergeant Waters' house. I am going to be watching his girls, but they will be sleeping, so it won't be hard. I want you to come, so I'm not alone. When I leave, it will be late at night."

He took a deep breath and raised his eyebrow.

"Okay, I guess." When we arrived, it was 9 P.M., and Sergeant Waters told us they were already in their rooms, and he had tucked them in, he had played a movie in their rooms, and they should be good. He said they would be back in a few hours.

As soon as Sergeant Waters' truck backed out of the driveway, I heard a loud thud and some crying. I hurried upstairs, afraid one of them had fallen out of bed and was hurt. Instead, I discovered they had escaped the makeshift baby gates. There were two in front of the door going down the hallway, and the last set of baby gates had been stacked three high in the door frame to have the kids stay in their rooms. Apparently, this was not a unique incident. They had scaled the fortress, and one was crying because she was stuck on it, while her sister had made it without her.

"What in the world?"

We tried to put them back in bed, but they kept coming out and scaling the gates, which seemed so dangerous, so we gave up and brought them downstairs. Stephen shook his head.

"He said that they would be in their rooms, but he never said they would not stay in their rooms. This is probably why he couldn't get a babysitter! Please don't volunteer me again."

I laughed and vowed never again.

It was an exhausting night. We could not get them to stay in bed or calm down. As soon as we put them down, they started over again. Stephen stayed with me even though it was exhausting, and even though they never went to sleep, they sat near him on the couch. He read them books, and he rocked the younger girl to calm her down. He was going to make a good dad someday, I mused. At 1:30 A.M., Sergeant Waters and his wife came strolling back in. Stephen handed the smallest girl, who could barely keep her eyes, open to her dad.

"So, I see why you had all those gates up! We couldn't get them to stay in bed!"

"Yes. They never really sleep, but I just put the TV on in there because otherwise, I would never sleep, since they barely sleep."

We left his house and made our way to our separate cars.

"Glad we got that out of the way. Please don't volunteer me again."

"I just wanted to see how you were with kids…"

"Yes, I realize that, and that's why I said okay."

I grinned. "You passed the test."

Chapel Duty & Extra Duty

This wouldn't be our last time watching kids together. We were pseudo aunt and uncle to some of our friends' kids, but we made sure we were unavailable for Sergeant Waters, never to be roped into babysitting for him again.

Chapter 8

The Eagle has Landed

Finally, we got word, after being without a chaplain, that a new one was inbound—Chaplain Eagle, who as over all of Fort Wainwright Unit Ministry Teams. He set up Monday meetings at his office at 10 A.M. sharp to meet with all the chaplains and chaplain assistants, so we could go over our mission and what was coming down the pipeline. He was a towering height, and he seemed reserved. His brown eyes squinted, and he smirked a lot, with folded hands as he nodded as others talked. I gathered from the weekly meetings that he expected people to get their work done quickly. He made it known that he planned on having teambuilding at some point, or what soldiers often refer to as "mandatory fun," events where we dressed in civilian clothes but were required to come to the function and participate in whatever they dreamed up.

Shortly after Chaplain Eagle's arrival, Chaplain Sword, who was going to become my direct supervisor, also arrived. He was the chaplain over the counseling center. It was a special assignment with extra train-

The Eagle has Landed

ing on counseling families. We had two interns who Chaplain Sword supervised who worked out of the center. Until the early 2000s, there was a saying in the Army: "If we wanted you to have a wife, we would have issued you one." The Army was realizing that without an intact family, the soldier was not "all in" and was not as effective or was not willing to continue in services while the family suffered. That's where Chaplain Sword came in. Chaplain Sword was in charge of the Family Counseling Center, adjacent from one of the chapels. Chaplain Sword was a sarcastic and funny guy who reminded me a lot of my dad. His crystal blue eyes glistened, as he told adventures that he had. He was a down-to-earth Southern gentleman who loved people well. Those same eyes always showed concern for those who whisked into the office, desperate, lonely, or needing hope. He had a calming presence and an ability to make people feel that, at that moment, what they were saying was the only important thing.

He asked me about my faith, my upbringing, and what I wanted to do after the Army, or if I wanted to make the Army a career. I was not sure, but I could see myself doing this for a while. He also asked who the installation chaplain was, because he wasn't around when he arrived on post.

"Sir, his name is Chaplain Eagle."

Chaplain Sword's left eyebrow raised, and a hint of recognition crossed his face.

"Oh, sir, you know him?" I asked. His lips twisted.

"Yes. I have worked with him before at Fort Bragg,"

"Sir?"

"Yes. Well, we will see how it goes, as we had a bit of history. I don't think he liked me telling him no," he explained

"How so, sir?"

"I had to speak up against a commander because of confidentiality, by not telling names of soldiers who were being counseled, so we butted heads a bit. Don't worry about that. It's water under the bridge, but at least I know what I'm getting into."

Upon meeting me and knowing I was his assigned chaplain assistant, as well as meeting the other single chaplain assistants, Chaplain Sword invited Stephen, Specialist Fox, and me over to his house to meet his family and have dinner. With Alaskan summers, the sun moved across the sky, but sunlight streamed in the window until 5 A.M. It didn't get dark in the summer, so we had plenty of daylight after the work day to get together. After mowing the lawn twice a week because it grew so much and Chaplain Sword wanted the greenest and best yard, I wasn't surprised that his yard was well kept. His house was close to the barracks we lived in, a five-minute car drive. His wife was inviting and warm, and he had a son and two daughters around my age. Chaplain Sword taught me how to cook a medium burger and season it to make it delicious. I became friends with his daughters, and we spent many weekends over at his house, as well as some weeknights for dinner.

On the day he sat down and said I was due my initial integration counseling, I was terrified. The only counseling I had gotten so far were from Sergeant Tiger, and no good had come of them. Chaplain Sword reassured me that this was to set the guideline and let us know how to work together, so it was a set of expectations for him and me. Education is very important to him, and he encouraged me and persuaded me to take college classes. He expected me to take initiative and told me it was important for building rapport with each other, so he liked to have me over at least once a month. If we deployed together, he wanted to feel as though we were on the same page. Chaplains in the Army are noncombatants, which means they are not to carry weapons by the standards

The Eagle has Landed

of the Geneva Convention. They are to minister to the people. A part of being a chaplain assistant is to protect the chaplain in a combat environment. He told me he wanted to make sure that I could shoot well. I assured him that I was a sharpshooter with my rifle, and I was sure I could get to an expert level with practice if we ever deployed. After a few months of growing to love his family, he stood in front of my desk one day, sipping his mug of Panamanian coffee. The warm, roasted beans wafted out from our coffee bar in the kitchenette area.

"Lorin, you are just about the same age as my daughters, and I am going to ask this question. Do you want me to treat you as one of my daughters or as a soldier?"

I smiled thinking he was kidding, but searching his eyes I realized he was serious.

"Sir, I love your family and respect you, but I am a soldier first."

The very first holiday I remember, Chaplain Eagle invited all the chaplains and chaplain assistants to his house, so everyone could get to know each other. His bubbly wife cooked delicious sweet potato casserole, which I had never had, and she had a sarcastic humor. Chaplain Eagle had a permanent smirk on his face, as if he knew a secret, but he was tighter than Fort Knox. He was a quiet and stilled presence in the background. He observed the people in the room, asking occasional questions. There were mostly guys there, as all of the soldiers were male except me, so I found my way to the island to chat with Chaplain Eagle's wife and daughter, Jessica, who was only two years younger than me.

The house had a cabin type feel, and the walls were adorned with mounted wildlife, deer, bear, wildcats, and moose antlers. It reminded me of an Elk Lodge I once saw in a movie. Stephen became startled by the bear around the edge of the living room. The bear was mounted as if it were in the middle of a fight, arms swinging, teeth bared, on the attack. Chaplain Eagle chuckled at him.

"Never seen one so close up, eh? Do you hunt or fish?" he asked.

"No, sir. I have never" was Stephen's reply.

"You have to do it. It's what men do. We are hunters. It's a rite of passage for my boys. You have to at least try some meat."

Stephen agreed he would give the bear stew a try, as he sat down in one of the chairs.

Chaplain Eagle moved next to Stephen.

"Well, if you don't hunt or fish, do you like sports?"

"Yes, sir. I'd usually rather play than watch."

"Do you play basketball?"

"Of course he does. He's black." Sergeant Waters offered.

The room laughed. Stephen looked sarcastically at him, and he cleared his throat.

"Well, yes, sir. I play basketball. I like a lot of sports, but I played football and ran track in school. I actually have many interests besides sports, like music."

Sergeant Waters, another chaplain assistant, spoke up. "I was surprised when I heard your rock music from your car the other day. You have to be the whitest black guy I know."

Then Sergeant Church piped in. "When I talked to you on the phone, I got to be honest, dude, I thought you were white."

Stephen shook his head.

"Yes, Sergeant. I remember that the first thing you said to me when you met me was, 'Oh… we didn't know you weren't white!'"

My cheeks flushed at the discussion. I mean, how stereotypical were they going to be? Also, what does it mean that someone doesn't sound black or do stereotypical black things? Are people not multifaceted?

"Yes. I used a professional voice, so you thought I couldn't be black?" Stephen challenged.

"No. Well, you know what I mean," Sergeant Church replied.

I wish I had said something at the time. I was embarrassed and shocked that they didn't see that my coworkers had essentially said that black people only spoke with slang words, and if people used Ebonics, they were less educated. They implied that black people only play basketball and listen to rap music. Sure, they were saying it a joking manner. Sure, it was a silly stereotype that he was good at basketball because he was black. Sure, it was just a joke. But the jokes only increased in frequency as time went on.

Another chaplain assistant even thought it was okay to call Stephen the N- word.

Stephen's nostrils flared, and his smiled disappeared, as he looked that chaplain assistant in his eyes. "Don't ever call me that again. It means ignorant, and I'm not."

"Hey! I didn't mean anything by it. My friends who are black are cool with me calling them that. It's a term of endearment," he defended.

"You don't know me, and I don't even use that word, so don't call me that, and we'll be just fine."

Unintentional or intentional, the sweeping generalizations, micro-aggressions, and racist comments had me questioning what I was doing here. I mean, I didn't understand the little jabs completely, but what did it mean that Stephen talked in his "work voice?" I asked him that later on in the night. He told me that sometimes black people do talk differently at work than outside of work. In order to be taken seriously, to be considered professional, they have to switch mannerisms to be perceived the least offensively.

"But, my mom just wanted me to talk with proper English, so I know how to do that, but I usually loosen up a bit around my friends."

The connection to different people allowed certain access to information. Some of the realizations I started to reach were ones I had some experience with. I had seen people behaving certain ways, but maybe I brushed it off, as that person didn't realize what they were doing. It had never seemed that obvious to me when I lived in New York. Then again, I am a white woman. I grew up in a predominantly white environment, and minorities were truly a small percentage of the people who surrounded me. Even thought I had friends of different backgrounds, I had not seen things, as I had begun to see then.

Another mandatory teambuilding adventure was ice fishing. I had never been ice fishing before because, frankly, I was not into fishing or being cold. Stephen and I, along with a chaplain assistant, Sergeant Tavy, rode in the back of my chaplain's truck with him. It took us about two hours to get to the lake, and we drove and slid on the ice and mounds of packed snow along the road, all while carrying my chaplain's four wheelers. I grabbed the door handle next to me and squealed when we slid. As soon as we made it to the lake, I thought we were going to park, but Chaplain Sword drove straight out onto the lake.

"Whoa, wait! Are we driving on the lake?"

The Eagle has Landed

Stephen looked as if he may get sick. Chaplain Sword chuckled.

"I take it you've never been ice fishin'? Don't worry. This is Alaska, and the lake has at least three or four feet of solid ice."

Stephen felt a little better, and I was just excited to get out of the truck. There were several little shacks on the lake that had smoke rising up out of them. If our fingers and toes felt numb, we could go in to warm up. There was a hole the size of a basketball drilled out in the middle where a fishing line with a hook was perched. All the chaplain assistants and chaplains tried our luck at fishing, but I gave up easily. I was ready to go four wheeling!

When I was in fifth grade, my parents bought me a used one from a neighbor, and I remembered how fun it was back home with friends, four wheeling occasionally. Stephen had never ridden one, but he picked it up quickly. Stephen and I were racing on the ice. The wind cut through my balaclava mask that surrounded my mouth and nose, so it only slapped against my eyes and part of my forehead. Some of the ice on the lake was bumpy, so when we hit a bump, the ATV flew into the air off the ice ramps, the shocks absorbing some of the impact as we landed and swerved out along the lake. Even though it was our whole team, I felt as if it was just him and I. My cheeks felt their first Alaskan windburn, and my eyebrows and eyelashes were adorned with icicles, but my heart felt as warm as those little warming huts on the ice.

Chapter 9

Grief

"The call of the Army Chaplain Corps is to nurture the living, care for the wounded, and honor the fallen."

-*U.S. Army Chaplain Corps*

There was the flurry and chaos that came from spouses carrying balloons, signs, and smiles in hand, all the wives dolled up, in the big aircraft hanger, waiting to see and hug their loved ones. The air was full of excitement and anticipation. A few moms toted a toddler on their hip, while others snuggled their newborn babies. Deployed husbands had just missed the birth, but they were about to meet their children for the first time! Deployed moms were about to be reunited with their kids and spouses! Suddenly, the Secretary of the Army stepped to the microphone with some news. When there was supposed to be laughter and joy, there was weeping, sorrow, and anger. To wait twelve months to land on U.S. soil, only to be told they will not be getting off to see their families, was the worst thing to hear. No, they were ordered back to the deployment

Grief

they thought they had survived and left behind. Worse still were the soldiers who had been home for a couple of weeks. They had a taste of being home again, and were then told to pack up again, as they were going back to the sandbox. The memorial services that happened during the last six months of the 172nd Infantry Brigade's deployment were the worst to endure. They were supposed to be home, and the heartbreak that ensued was horrible.

As chaplain assistants, we did a lot of clerical and managerial type tasks, coordination and scheduling of events, and a lot of background type work. We were in the business of helping in all aspects of caring for soldiers and their families. Memorials are a significant part of the job. We helped fix video montages of the soldiers who were lost, of their families, of their fellow brothers and sisters in arms. Then we set up the memorial stand and got the chapel ready to receive the influx of people. We also helped with some peer counseling and held a space for people. I had made plans to see one of my friends from basic training, but I never got to. I lost my friend, Phelps, stationed out of Anchorage. He was a paralegal and had gotten hit with an IED. It always hurt to hear we were holding a memorial service in the chapel, but the closer you are to the person, the harder it stings. I held a parishioner from our Catholic congregation, as she mourned the loss of her husband. I never met him, but I knew their family well. I watched the names of the deceased scroll down the screen in the chapel. Sometimes, it was a memorial service for multiple soldiers at a time.

Though it is a tragic and solemn event, there is something beautiful and magical that happens in a military community. No matter what differences may exist politically or religiously, the entire community always rallies around.

One of the worst case scenarios for a military family is when two officers show up at a doorstep. One of those officers is the chaplain. They read off the script to inform you that your loved one is deceased, to say they are sorry, but your soldier will not come home.

Often the chaplain gives the eulogy at the memorials. Some chaplains don't know the soldier but they gather information from family members and friends. They allowed us to see a snapshot of their lives, to tell the story of where they came from and of their hearts to serve, as well as other stories of that person. It helps it become more personal when you can put a story to the name and face.

Many people came to pay their respects and show solidarity, even if they didn't know the deceased soldier. They were still precious souls whose lives were cut short. Most of the memorial services I worked for had soldiers who were in the infantry and in the range of eighteen to twenty-three years old. These were my peers. That could have been me. I have always been an emotional person, but I allowed myself to cry and mourn the precious lives as fully as I could. Tears streamed down my face and tasted salty as I licked my lips, as I tried to pull myself together, as I ran the soundboard or slide show. Even if I wasn't running the sound board, I made it a point to sit in on the eulogy. I helped usher people to seats, stocked up the tissue boxes, and handed out tissues. The hardest part of the memorial service is always at the end.

The unit does the final roll call. Roll call is taken during formation. The roll call is calling out the people in the company, including the name of the deceased, with their names being called out three times. By the third time the soldier's name is called, chills shot up through my spine. That is when it sets in that the soldier is not answering. The soldier is no longer with us. The family there is wailing, and the sounds of mourning are unforgettable. Hundreds of people, crammed into the sanctuary and overflow seating in the vestibule, mourn the loss of their friend, their brother, their comrade. Some just mourn the loss of a person, serving our country, something that less than one percent of the population ever

Grief

does. Soldiers and civilians come together to pay honor and tribute. There is rarely a dry eye. What follows the call is the twenty-one gun salute. The sound of fire echoes outside the walls of the chapel, then Reveille resounds. Twenty one shots sound from the seven-man honor guard, firing three times, each time echoing through the loudspeakers on post. The flag is then lowered to honor at half mast.

The only thing more gut wrenching than the final roll call and taps was watching people pay their last respects. Memorial attendees and fellow soldiers wait in line. They wait in the middle aisle for their turn to be face to face with the memorial stand. The memorial stand is comprised of a pair of combat boots, set at a forty-five-degree angle as if standing at attention, an M-16 assault rifle vertically placed, with the Kevlar (soldier's protective helmet) balanced on top, as the soldier's dog tags dangle down the rifle. A sizable picture frame with a photo of the soldier stands on one side, with floral arrangements on the other. I saw brothers and sisters in arms, each go up to the memorial. I saw their lips move, and some cried out, some said a prayer, and others signed the cross. Hands grasped, and some rubbed the engraved dog tag with the owner's full name and social that draped down. I came completely undone. I had never deployed, but each face from the hundreds of memorial service programs, ones I folded by hand, still scrolls through my mind from time to time.

I don't ever want to forget. I want to honor their memory. What a sacrifice it was, these soldiers who died, who went down fighting alongside their friends, their Army family, their unit.

We were in Alaska, so most of the funerals were done in the lower forty-eight, the states that are the continental U.S. The few times that soldiers' families were from Alaska, we did funerals. Most are closed caskets because the families would rather remember soldiers as they were and not what remained after an IED explosion or a gunshot wound. The purple hearts and triangular folded flags given the next of kin, the spouse or the children, were enough to crack the hardest hearts into blubbering messed. How do you explain to children that their moms or dads weren't coming home? Never again. It's a hard and sobering reality.

My condolences and prayers seemed as if they were not enough to honor my fellow soldiers. I pleaded with God on their behalf. I wrestled with it, and sometimes still do, when soldiers I know pass away or when veterans take their own lives because of the horrors of war. To be honest, I don't think I'll ever understand this side of Heaven. Where I find solace and comfort is from my Maker. He cares about the crushed spirit, and those who feel weary will be given rest. I may never understand what I have witnessed, the heartache others have endured more so than me, but what I know is that God catches every tear I ever cried. He can do the same for anyone.

I learned in real time how precious life is, how I need to make the most of every second I have. I learned how to tell people I love them when they are here, and I learned how to love fully with abandon. Our days are numbered, and I was reminded to make every moment count.

Chapter 10

Falling

"Two people are better than one because together they have a good reward for their hard work. If one falls the other can help his friend get up. But how tragic it is for the one who is all alone when he falls."

(Ecclesiastes 4:9-12, NLT)

Alaska was incredibly beautiful. Sparkling white snowflakes glistened on the ground, and snow and ice crystallized on the trees. Stephen and I got to marvel at the wonder of the aurora borealis (northern lights), as the breathtaking art show of green swirls danced across the night sky. God had taken a paintbrush and swirled a perfect abstract picture. No description or picture could ever truly do its majesty justice, as it gleamed in front of us. We watched a part of the Iditarod (the famous dogsled race) drove to the town of Denali, nestled in the mountains, to see Mount McKinley. We ventured to the Santa Claus house, complete with real reindeer and the jolly ol' elf himself in North Pole, Alaska. We encountered a near disastrous run-in, getting in between a moose and its baby. We drove ATVs (all terrain vehicles) along the trails. We drifted his souped-up Ford Focus with rally stripes on a track made after a lake had frozen over. We drifted with friends in empty parking lots, just for fun, and we learned how to drive in Alaskan winters, just as recommended in the newcomer's brief from the military police. Stephen and I experienced the wonder of the Chena Hot Springs, a natural hot spring that made me marvel at creation, yet also turned up my nose as it smelled of sulfur. The Chena Hot Springs trip was a special trip as part of the marriage ministry retreats we worked on as chaplains and chaplain assistants. However, the memories I love are so wrapped up in the ordinary everyday moments and bloopers.

Watching people fall on post, as they slipped and skidded on ice, was hilarious and a favorite pastime. We were entertained, as we laughed at our live-action show during our lunch breaks. I worked near the welcome center, the administrative building that all new soldiers had to frequently visit as they were processed into their new units. I loved watching people, as the new troops looked like newborn baby deer on wobbly legs, unsure, having just arrived into this strange world. To no avail, soldiers struggled to walk or run, and they wiped out on the ice and snow. When it was a good fall, they sometimes took others down with them, almost as if they were bowling for people. Everyone knew how to identify who the new soldiers were in Alaska. They took giant steps or attempted to run on the ice. Without proper gear like Yaktrax, which contain metal wiring that connect to boots to give some traction, they are doomed to fall. The correct way to operate in Alaskan snow was to use the Alaskan shuffle. The Alaskan shuffle is where you don't pick your feet up the entire way, but sort of shuffle your feet as you walk, dragging your feet back and forth in small increments.

I know it seems mean, but I laugh at myself when I fall, too. It was

Falling

a rite of passage that every soldier new to Alaska had to acclimate to. I remember, after my first snowfall, I put on some sexy red pumps, thinking that I looked like a finalist on American's Next Top Model— Tyra would have been proud. I sauntered down the hall of my barracks and stepped out to the parking lot. Promptly, I fell down all five stairs and then slid down the entire span of the sidewalk into the parking lot. I cracked up, searching for any bystanders who witnessed my folly, as I rubbed my sore back and bruised ego. I went back inside and put on my mismatching, yet practical, Alaska Army-issued black winter boots. Whenever you think you're too hot to trot, God can bring you down a few notches. On a practical level, I learned to bring my shoes to change into, if I wanted to pull together my look without the risk of falling.

When Stephen first got to Alaska, he became aware of the difference between Alaskan winter gear and that of the lower forty-eight (what Alaskans refer to as the other states in the continental U.S.). Texas winter coats were not going to cut it for Alaskan winters, no matter how puffy the jacket was. Layers and insulated boots were the key to keeping warm. All cars and trucks in Alaska had to be winterized and plugged into electrical outlets, so the battery didn't freeze. They had to equip your car with a trickle charger or a battery warmer. Alaska's coldest temperature we faced was a numbing negative seventy degrees. To understand what that's like, imagine a cold that just hurts your face, and icicles forming on your eyebrows and eyelashes. Soldiers tell you not to swipe them, or your eyelashes could break off!

Poor Stephen did not get the memo of the importance of Alaskan boots. What did he know, coming from Texas? We had gone to Chili's, as that was one of our only comfort food restaurants, and Stephen was wearing a pair of fashionable, Texas acceptable, winter boots. He couldn't gain traction and kept landing on his back. Smack on his back, it happened again, BAM, again, BAM, and again. Every time he got back up, he returned to the crisp snow-packed ground of the parking lot. After about the seventh time, I was nearly peeing my pants. I laughed so hard that my shoulders were shaking, and no sounds were coming out. Trying to talk as I gasped for air, I asked if I could help him up.

Embarrassed from falling again and again, he said, "Garbage! No, I got it!" I watched as he, for the last time, got up to his feet. His boots flew straight up in the air and over his head, looking like a wrestling move where someone had picked him up and slammed him down. Ouch!

"Are you sure you don't want some help? You are in the middle of the parking lot. I don't want you to get run over."

"I need a moment. I'm just gonna lie here a few minutes and collect my thoughts."

Life can be the best teacher of experiences. Not too surprisingly, the next day, I accompanied him, as we went shopping for some winter boots and quality winter gear.

While we were in the midst of the Alaskan winter and continually falling on the ice, I was in the process of falling in love with my best friend. Stephen was everything I had imagined love to be, as well as some of what I didn't know I needed. He didn't shy away from the truth, but he knew me and loved me, despite my imperfections.

A Japanese proverb says, "Fall seven times. Rise eight." When I found soul-to-soul connections in my friendship, then in love, I felt invincible. It's a lot easier in life to get back up when we have someone extending a hand out to us. These are the friendships where you walk beside each other and cheer each other on, motivating each other forward when we feel we can't take one more step. In life, we will fall. I would say in my own experience, it's more like falling ninety-nine times and still pushing my bruised ego and tattered body to stand up, just one more time.

Chapter 11

Family Visits

My grandma and aunt from my dad's side of the family planned a cruise trip to Alaska and had to stop in to see their favorite soldier—me. Once they made their way to the minor city of Fairbanks, we went to the Santa Claus House, and I showed them where I worked and lived. We enjoyed Alaskan tourist adventures together, one being gold panning. I was so hyped up that I might strike it rich, like an old prospector from an old Western movie. However, all I found with all my hard work was some gold flakes. I'm sure whoever owned the mine filtered it out for any actual chunks of gold ahead of tme, and we had to pay for experience and the weight in gold. They got to meet Stephen, and my aunt kept thinking his name was Steamin' instead of Stephen. It was a wonderful time, but having that taste of home made me miss my family, and I especially missed my little sister.

My sister and I are almost six years apart. We grew up getting along pretty well because we were always in different stages of life, so we didn't have that normal sister rivalry. When I was in basic training, my sweet sister wrote me encouraging letters. It seemed every day I got a letter, and we grew even closer. I wanted her to meet Stephen because even though she was younger than me, she had an old, wise soul and was a good judge of character. She could discern things. I wanted her to come see me in Alaska, meet Stephen, and have some sister time and an adventure. I begged my parents to let my then fifteen-year-old sister fly by herself to me to stay two weeks during the summer, and I would take care of her. They reluctantly agreed.

I took Army leave (vacation time), and since I didn't have a bunch of money to spend on a hotel stay, I snuck her into the barracks to stay with me. It was most definitely against the rules to have an under-aged person in the barracks.

In previous relationships, I had tried to be agreeable to a fault and never wanted to ruffle feathers. Unfortunately, Stephen had also experienced being taken advantage of, so when we began our relationship, we decided we would put it all on the table. Whatever we believed in was laid out, so we wouldn't hold back, and we were both stubborn. It was that way since the beginning. At times, I doubted the "staying power" of our relationship because I wondered if two people who were wired so differently could last with all the conflict.

My poor teenage sister was a witness to these disagreements. Alas, she was stuck with us, driving down to Anchorage during the first weekend of her stay. We were relentless and arguing the whole time, about everything and anything.

"I just want to get there. Why are we making so many stops!" I demanded.

"I had to get gas and then use the bathroom. Can you relax?" he retorted.

Family Visits

It has always triggered me when someone tells me to relax. "I don't need to relax. I need you to hurry up."

As we navigated down the winding Denali pass, I felt queasy.

"You are making me car sick. Can you take it easy on the turns?"

"I'm driving the best as I can. These roads are winding."

After being queasy, the last thing I wanted to listen to was loud guitar riffs. My stomach was queasy, and I was irritable and snapped.

"Can we listen to something else, please?"

"Why can't you ask without biting my head off? I can change it, but you need to change your attitude!"

"Don't tell me what to do! You could change your driving, and that would change how I feel and my attitude."

Lianne tried to distract us and deflect from arguing in the car with the occasional, "Wow! Look at that!"

Stephen and I stopped, taking in the beautiful landscape of the Denali Pass. They shut it down in the winter because of the weather, but during the summer, it was a busy place. Then after a little bit, we started arguing again. The trip to Anchorage took seven hours. Seven hours of mostly bickering. Seven hours of carsickness. My sister is a saint. After we checked into the Air Force lodging where we were staying, our argument continued to include something about the room. We wandered the mall attached to the theater. My future husband paused to fix his collar of his red polo in the store. The store clerk followed Stephen around.

"Can I help you?"

"No. I'm just looking." The clerk followed him like a puppy dog, and

Stephen couldn't take one step back without bumping into him.

"Can I help you now?" the clerk pressed.

"Forget it! I'm leaving." What the workers hadn't known is that my sister and I could hear them talking back and forth on their headset, saying they should follow him because he looked suspicious. Suspicious was wearing a red polo, fitted jeans, and being black? He was respectful and looked everyone in the eye who talked to him. I couldn't help notice. One followed me around or has ever followed me around.

"You know how they are. Keep a close eye on him and his sticky fingers. He probably can't afford our prices."

I was indignant. I rushed out of the store.

"Has that happened to you before? Because I only imagined those things to be in movies." Sure, there was discrimination in New York, but in my experience, it seemed more subtle, the kind that had you questioning if it could be. However, racism and prejudice reared its ugly face and made it so unmistakable to be chalked up to anything else. Even if our families were cool with our relationship, not all were.

We made our way back to the theater to finalize our movie selection and grab some popcorn before our movie started. We argued about what movie we were going to see, whether we needed the extra butter, and then continued bickering in our chairs. I loathed the movie. It was a terrible choice with terrible acting, and I was over it as soon as it started. I used my elbow to weasel my arm to get the armrest I felt I deserved.

"Hey! Use the other armrest. I want this one."

"No. You use the other one. I want both."

My sister stood up, exasperated. "Will you two stop it? You have been fighting all day! Now that's it!"

Family Visits

She motioned for me to change spots, and, sighing, she plopped down between us, separating us.

We laughed a lot on the way home, joking about feeling like two little kids who were reprimanded.

"You guys seem to fight because you are both stubborn and want to be heard, but you don't always have to agree on things. Maybe you should work on listening to each other." Now we had to navigate how to fight fairly, to listen to understand, not just to plan a rebuttal, to disagree and hash it out. Yes, we loved each other, but we needed to learn how to love and work through conflict.

Chapter 12

Fraternizing

"4–14 b. Relationships between Soldiers of different rank are prohibited if they— (1) Compromise, or appear to compromise, the integrity of supervisory authority or the chain of command. (2) Cause actual or perceived partiality or unfairness. (3) Involve, or appear to involve, the improper use of rank or position for personal gain. (4) Are, or are perceived to be, exploitative or coercive in nature. (5) Create an actual or clearly predictable adverse impact on discipline, authority, morale, or the ability of the command to accomplish its mission. c. Certain types of personal relationships between officers and enlisted personnel are prohibited. Prohibited relationships include— (1) Ongoing business relationships between officers and enlisted personnel. (2) Dating, shared living accommodations other than those directed by operational requirements, and intimate or sexual relationships between officers and enlisted personnel. This prohibition does not apply to— (a) Marriages. When evidence of fraternization between an officer and enlisted member prior to their marriage exists, their marriage does not preclude appropriate command action based on the prior fraternization. Com-

Fraternizing

manders have a wide range of responses available including counseling, reprimand, order to cease, reassignment, administrative action or adverse action. Commanders must carefully consider all of the facts and circumstances in reaching a disposition that is appropriate. Generally, the commander should take the minimum action necessary to ensure that the needs of good order and discipline are satisfied. (b) Situations in which a relationship that complies with this policy would move into non-compliance due to a change in status of one of the members (for instance, a case where two enlisted members are dating and one is subsequently commissioned or selected as a warrant officer). In relationships where one of the enlisted members has entered into a program intended to result in a change in their status from enlisted to officer, the couple must terminate the relationship permanently or marry within either one year of the actual start date of the program, before the change in status occurs, or within one year of the publication date of this regulation, whichever occurs later."*

    Sergeant Church started to notice there was something between us, maybe the look of admiration in my eyes, and, unfortunately, so did Chaplain Eagle. Immediately, we were summoned to his office to talk. Sergeant Church cleared his throat.
"I know you guys seem to like each other, but starting in a few days, Specialist Hayes, Chaplain Eagle is going to put you over the chapel and the family life center."

I protested, "But I work there, Sergeant! How will that work?"
"Oh you still will work there, but Specialist Hayes will be in charge of both areas of operation. This means you guys better stop whatever it is that's between you before it starts. Starting now, you are her supervisor and need to keep it professional."
Stephen protested, "Sergeant, we are already seeing each other, and this doesn't make sense."
"Sorry." Then he turned to look at me.
"I tried to warn you, Whiteman, not to mess with him."

---

* Army Regulations 600-20, section 4-14. 2014.

For the first time in a while, I was truly happy, and now I felt like an elephant was on my chest. It was hard to breathe. I went to my room, as tears streamed down my face.

We decided to try to do what they said. We still hung out. We were best friends first, so we were constantly together. We worked together, as I showed him how we ran programs and the outdated SOP (standard of operation) of the chapel, and we were together after work hours. Not seeing each other romantically lasted all of four days.
"I can't do this! I like you. I am attracted to you. I want to date you," I lamented to him.
"I know," he said. "I tried to talk to Sergeant Church again, but it seems they are determined to put me over you. Chaplain Eagle keeps telling Sergeant Church if anything goes wrong and we don't work out, we could ruin the morale of the unit and of the chaplain section. How awkward it would be if we have those feelings of not liking each other, yet have to work so closely together."

Stephen and I decided to date, regardless of Church's words. We weren't big on public displays of affection anyway, and we were always together, so we picked dating back up, this time secretly. As time went on, we could feel the disdain for Stephen seemed to rise.

Chaplain Eagle put Stephen in for a special promotion to corporal, since he was in charge and a specialist. Why not just help him be promoted to sergeant? Well, there was an Army point system for promotion, and one had to have enough points to be promoted. Chaplain assistant promotions usually came up maybe once or twice a year when the E-7s, or Sergeant First Class soldiers, could be promoted, and then their current slots become available. There needs to be open slots for people to be eligible to be promoted, so the points were usually the highest they could be, except for about twice a year. This seemed like a nice gesture, but there aren't many corporals in the Army. The only exception to this is in the infantry units, where the title of corporal could be useful being a squad leader. It could put you into a leadership role, as well as the same rank as those in the squad. There is not one chaplain assistant who has been a corporal, as far as I know. It is unnecessary, and one can work within two ranks of the current rank, but, as Hayes pointed out, then he would be a Jr. NCO (Junior Noncommissioned Officer, thus legally unable to date me, according to Army regulations).

Fraternizing

Chaplain Eagle wasn't fond of someone challenging his orders when Stephen respectfully said, " It's illegal, unmoral, and unethical. I don't have to do it."

Sergeant Church called Stephen.
"We got a new chaplain assistant, and we need you to follow him from his house to anywhere he goes and then report back because Eagle doesn't think he's working."
"No, Sergeant."
"You can't tell me no. That's a direct order."
"Sergeant, if it's illegal, immoral, or unethical, I don't have to do it."
Sergeant Church hung up the phone.
Stephen called me.
"Listen. I need to tell you something quick. Sergeant Church is going to call you and ask for something ridiculous and illegal. You should tell him no when he calls."

"Okay. Thanks."

My phone rang a minute later.
"Listen. I need you to do a favor for Chaplain Eagle. We need someone to follow Specialist Sam to make sure that he is where he says."
"No, Sergeant. I'm not going to do that."
"What? You can't tell me no! It's an order!"
"Sergeant, I can say no if it's illegal, immoral, or unethical."
"Wait a minute. Hayes called you, didn't he?"

We were reprimanded. Stephen told me not to worry because they couldn't make us do illegal things. Chaplain Eagle recruited another solider for the "secret mission." Sam told us he saw Fox and was ready to fight him, as he was following him everywhere, even to his wife's doctor's appointment. He could have gotten into legal trouble if Sam had pursued it.

I was glad that I started to question orders and rules that were spouted at me. Up until I met Stephen, I blindly believed that the people above me knew more than me and also were doing the right thing, without question. The veil had been removed from my eyes.

Every single extra duty assignment was handed to Stephen. He worked as a postal worker in the on-post mail unit, ran the official mail for our unit, was in charge of taking care of the company vehicles, and he was tasked out for anything. If someone had a need, Hayes was tasked with accomplishing it. He became the driver for important visitors on post. He was still also expected to do the normal chaplain assistant duties as well of maintaining the facilities, and covering events. He also worked at the hospital to help the hospital chaplain with taking care of soldiers, he spoke at the new incoming soldier's brief, he taught the suicide prevention trainings, and he supported the Family Readiness Groups. He was going in early and staying late, nearly every day.

My direct chaplain was able to run some interference for me because he needed someone to run the front desk, so they couldn't always get me for these extra duties, but Stephen was not assigned a chaplain, so he had no built-in protection.

The company commander of the post and the sergeant major took notice of Stephen. He was wearing so many hats, and he had positive energy. They recognized him for his outstanding work ethic, for, just as the Army says, "embracing the suck," even with all the stuff Chaplain Eagle piled on, he had a good attitude and worked hard.

I think when Chaplain Eagle realized that maybe a promotion might also be good for Stephen, he started to regret the paperwork that he had sent in for him to be a corporal. There had to be a justifiable reason to remove his name from the special promotion, and one day, Chaplain Eagle found his "justifiable" way out.
The blotter came out on post for any infraction that occurred. Stephen received a speeding ticket on base, which was contested and dismissed in court as invalid. However, Chaplain Eagle claimed to be because Stephen's ticket was on the blotter, and he was not made aware of it ahead of time. He did not care that the charge was invalid.
"You won't be a corporal anymore. Forget about being promoted!"

Chapter 13

Unconventional Dating

Stephen and I were constantly together, mostly in group settings. We enjoyed hanging out with people, and we also had to keep up our appearance of being "just friends." One of the most unforgettable memories in Alaska was a trip with our friends to go snowboarding and skiing at the ski lodge. The first time we went, I stuck to the bunny hill, as I was not a novice, and thought bunny hill was best, with most of the skiers on it being little children. Some of our friends, however, were no strangers to snowboarding.

He decided that after maybe two times down the bunny hill with his snowboard, he was ready for the real deal. He went to join our friends on the regular slope. He gained confidence as he maintained his balance, so he got braver. Stephen shot off a ramp where he landed on his feet. "Alright! Ooh, baby, did you see that?" Yes he landed on his feet, but what he neglected to learn at the bunny hill was how to stop.

Stephen was gaining speed, as he barreled down the hill, and his snowboard crossed into the bunny hill area. He knocked a little boy over, flailing his arms, screaming, "Sorry! Get out the way! I can't stop!"

I laughed so much, that I leaned back and plopped into the snow with my snowboard attached, as he gained speed like a snowball rolling down the hill. People jumped out of the way, diving left and right. His eyes were drying even though he had goggles. He yelled, "Move out the way!" There was a grade at the bottom of the slope. It made him turn right where there was a snowbank, a mound about fifteen feet tall. He was heading right toward the glass of the lodge, as a crowd inside pressed their faces to the glass. "AHHH!" he screamed.

Luckily for Stephen, the mound made it so at the very last minute, he turned and didn't crash. Unfortunately, instead of having him go up the incline and come back down to slow to a stop, it acted more like a ramp. He flew off the packed snow and ice, through the parking lot, his momentum still going strong, and he was not stopping. At that point, he was headed directly into the skeet range. As he flew into the range, they called for a cease fire, and he threw himself back, sliding on his back, toward oncoming skeet range firers.

By that time, I had detached my snowboard and was too far away to help him, but I saw some of the chaos. As his snowboard caught the ice, he spun in circles like a turtle on its shell. He went to the end of the skeet range where the clay plates flew through the air. He continued on, spinning on his back, into the parking lot. A car had the nerve to honk its horn at him. There was never a dull moment, just like the very first one-on-one date.

Since most of our dates were more like hanging out among our group of friends or staying in to watch a movie, Stephen wanted to do something different with just the two of us.

Unconventional Dating

"I have a surprise date planned for you," he revealed to me.

"What is it? You need to tell me!"

Most people are excited to have a surprise, but I hate surprises. I hate that feeling of knowing something is up but not knowing what it is. We had just begun dating, and Stephen and I watched movies together or ate out, but more often in group settings, to keep up our "just friends" facade.

"I can't tell you. I have to show you."

We drove in his silver blue striped rally car, winding up a steep mountain.

"Is there a cute restaurant up here?" I asked.

"It's a surprise. You'll see."

I saw nothing but the woods.

Every ten minutes, he pulled over, got out, and said, "Nope. Not here."

As time went on, I was antsy.

"Where are we going? What are we doing here?"

"It's a surprise," he repeated.

My mind drove me on a trip of its own. We were up in the middle of nowhere, and there was no cell phone signal, there were no cars, no houses that I could see, nothing.

"Nope. Not here."

Oh my GOD! Is he going to kill me? Did he plan a spot where he arranged to kill me? Great… I'm going to be buried in the middle of the woods, and he's looking for the spot where all his murdering weapons and tools are strategically waiting! I gripped the handle on the door.

Finally, we stopped at a clearing. It was dusk, but I could see we were at the top of a mountain at a lookout point.

"You've got to be kidding me! We missed it," he lamented.

"What?"

"I wanted to show you this beautiful view, but maybe we can look at the stars instead."

Stephen was trying so hard to remember where it was, as he had accidentally found it driving one day and wanted us to see the sunset together. The problem was, the sun had long been set. It frustrated him, and the surprise was ruined. He climbed out of the car, and he rushed around the car to open my door. I slapped a mosquito on my leg, then two more on my arm. I squashed another three. I looked over and saw Stephen battling his own mosquitoes. Our eyes locked, but when they met, we realized there was a whole swarm of mosquitos. They chased us around the car. These mosquitoes weren't just the run-of-the-mill mosquitoes. They were Alaska-sized mosquitoes. The joke in Alaska is that mosquitos are the state bird. We ran around the perimeter of the car, trying to lose the swarm, yelling and swatting.

"Quick! Get in," he shouted. We jumped back into the car. "So much for the surprise. I'm sorry."

I chuckled. "Thank God this was the surprise. I thought you might want to kill me."

We spent the next ten minutes squishing mosquitos off our bodies that had followed us inside the car, and we laughed deep belly laughs.

In the following months, Stephen and I were inseparable. We worked together, we hung out together outside of work, and we played on our unit's basketball and softball teams.

Our unit had finished our practice for our softball game. Someone threw a glove at my new Jeep, and it thudded on the passenger side door as I was driving away. I slammed my car into park and jumped out of the car, leaving my door wide open.

"What the hell?" I demanded. "Who threw that?"

Fox laughed, and I drew back and punched him in his arm.

He returned my blow with a little more force than I initially did. My eyes grew.

"I can't believe you just punched me!"

"It was only my glove, and if you're going to punch me, I'm going to punch you back even harder."

I balled my fists, and I punched him again in his arm. No one was going to start something and think that I was going to stand there and take it.

He punched me harder.

I yelled. I drew my arm back, ready to give it my best. Stephen had seen our altercation and scurried over to us to put his body in between us.

"Hey! Don't hit her. Do not touch her, or you will have to deal with me," he threatened.

"She hit me first!"

"You threw something at my car when I was driving." I gritted my teeth. I glared at Fox, waiting for his response.

"I just think of you as my little sister," he defended.

"I'm not your sister. Don't ever do that to me again!"

Fox apologized. I am pretty sure it was because Stephen was standing there.

Stephen turned off the car's engine, closed my door, and gently guided me back toward the field to calm down.

A few months earlier, Stephen helped negotiate a trade for my car, an early 2000s sky blue Jeep that I adored. It was perfect for this nice summer weather, as well as the ice and snow of Alaskan winters. Stephen helped me grow in my knowledge and appreciation of cars.

I have always appreciated car knowledge, as my dad has owned his share of muscle cars over the years, and he works on them mainly himself. My dad had taught me years ago to change a tire, but growing up, he had always been there to do it for me. I never actually needed to change a tire on my own, nor did I have the desire.

A few days after that practice, I ran over a nail, and my tire went flat. I was told by my supervisor that they didn't care how, but I better get myself to where I needed to be. I didn't have the money for a tow truck, and I didn't know what I could do. Stephen came with a jack and handed me the tire iron.

"Can't you just do this for me? I don't want to do it."

"I will help you, but I want you to be able to do this in case you ever have to do it without me there."

I rolled my eyes and grumbled. I had to get this done quickly, and I was in no mood to learn. Together, we installed the spare tire. I had to admit, it felt good to be able to do it.

Stephen met me later that day, at the Autoskills Center, a self-service garage on post, to remove the nail and plug the hole to fix my tire. As we paid for using the vehicle bay, we overheard a woman corralling a busy toddler, pleading with the receptionist to help her.

"My husband is deployed, and I don't know how to do any of this! I don't have anyone to watch my son, or even if I could get someone to watch him, I don't know how to put the tires on. Isn't there anyone who can help me?" Stephen stepped in and helped her. Following him was an additional three soldiers who stopped working on their cars to join in. When Stephen went to finish paying for our bay, he discreetly paid her bill.

Stephen cared about people and serving others, but what made me feel even more special is that although he took care of me, he also believed in me and empowered me. Stephen pushed me to do things for myself and never gave me the easy way out. I never felt as if I was behind him or dragging him along, but that we walked beside each other as equals.

Chapter 14

Paradise

One of my favorite memories from our time dating was when we were able to visit paradise. We were able to take a hop (free military flight) to Hawaii from Eielson Air Force Base. We were both single soldiers who participated in the BOSS program, which stood for Better Opportunities for Single Soldiers. With twelve spots available for this trip, Sergeant Major had to randomly pick two soldiers to go, and he designated Stephen and me. I was excited that Stephen and I could get a chance to go to Hawaii's warm tropical breezes, a stark contrast from the negative seventy degree weather we were having in Alaska. That was the kind of cold where it just hurts to go outside, or your eyelashes and eyebrows get ice on them, just from stepping outside. That was the kind of cold where I shoveled four times a day, making a pathway to the counseling center, when all the snowblowers broke down again. Yes! I needed some warm weather for these bones! We loaded onto a full flight.

The pilot stood and made an announcement.

Paradise

"We need someone to stay behind from BOSS because we have someone who is going on emergency leave who needs a spot. Is anyone willing to give up their seat?"

We need someone to get off the flight from our group because of priority level. My eyes snapped toward Stephen, knowing he's both a gentleman and kindhearted, and I whispered, "Don't raise your hand. Don't even look in that direction!"

The only person who knew Stephen and I volunteered begrudgingly. When she left, Stephen and I could let our guard down.

I've never been a good flyer, but in the C130, only the pilot cabin was pressurized. The seats we flew on were something straight out of the Saving Private Ryan movie. These aircraft are not created for comfort—they are created for function. Everyone sat in cargo net seats, there were no seatbelts, and all of our luggage was piled in the middle and roped off, so it didn't roll everywhere. The whistle of the air and ferocity of the takeoff, along with any turbulence, caused me to ball up, holding my popping ears. I tried all my usual tricks—chewing gum, popping my ears, gulping to swallow to pop my ears—all to no avail. An Army doctor who was flying with us was concerned for me and checked me out. I got to go into the pilot cabin while we were landing, so my poor ears could have a break, and it was the most beautiful view I have ever experienced—watching as the islands called us in and the water glimmered, sparkling turquoise and blue, inviting us to the shore.

When you get to take a trip on a hop, the trip is done by priority. Instead of first class, the priority went to active duty soldiers who might be going on emergency leave for a family member's death, all the way down to someone on leave (vacation time). We were third in priority as a TDY because we were going to learn about Pearl Harbor and to check out the USRR Arizona. It was chilling. We walked onto that ship, knowing that some soldiers are still, to this day, trapped below in the deep blue sea. I cried a lot, thinking of those brave soldiers who died that day. While it was an emotionally exhausting day, we did get to plan the next day at the beach.

Hawaiian locals thought we were crazy for getting in the water. It was seventy degrees that second day, but we had come from negative seventy degrees, so we were frolicking in the water and splashing each other. Day three led us on a snorkeling adventure. It was beautiful, with coral and fish that freaked Stephen out a bit when they rushed by our legs. I laughed so much during the trip. Wow, this is what Hawaii is like? I loved everything about it, expect for the traffic. It took three hours to get twenty minutes down the shore in the rush hour traffic. If I had been stationed in Hawaii, I most likely would have been deployed, and then would never have met Stephen. God places us exactly where we need to be, even when we don't think we want to be there. I would have never met Stephen.

Not only is Hawaii incredibly beautiful, but it holds a soft spot in my heart because it was the first time we held hands in public. Virtually no one knew us in Hawaii because the other soldiers were from different units in Alaska, so we held hands, he put his arm around me, and it was as if we were a normal couple. I didn't want to leave paradise to go back to the icy tundra of Fairbanks. We walked a lot, even in the city, and we spotted Dog the Bounty Hunter while we were out, which was hilarious to the guys in our group. The group decided to go out dancing, and we went to a Hawaiian club. Guests had to have collared shirts to enter the club, so we went on an excursion to find polos for a few of the guys in our group who were in T-shirts. When we got back to the entrance, Stephen and I exchanged glances.

Stephen is more of an introvert, and the crowd and club scene wasn't his thing. I hadn't had much experience because I was too young to go anywhere in Alaska, so I was excited! I had a blast dancing the

Paradise

night away with Stephen. My face hurt from smiling so much, and he was horrified when I was entranced by a girl dancing. "What is she doing? Wait… how does she get her butt to do that?" Stephen tried hard to guard his eyes so as not to look. "Lorin, please stop gaping at her."

"But, how does she do that? What are the mechanics behind it? Does she practice in front of a mirror?"

I had seen music videos but never in person like that.

We were lucky enough to stay one extra day because the flight was canceled, as the training plane had to take a mission-essential trip. One more day of bliss. One more day of just me and Stephen, strolling hand in hand. A week of seeing how normal life could be, him putting his arm around me. This trip solidified that not only did I love Stephen, but being friends with someone first made it so that we laughed and enjoyed each other's company. I did not want to leave this tropical paradise… ever. It was like a honeymoon phase after a wedding. There was no arguing, just paradise and bliss.

As we boarded the hop to head back to Fairbanks, I felt sorrow and wondered how we were going to be together when we were going back to real life. As my ears burned with the non-pressurized cabin, tears stung my eyes, but this time not from the pain of my ears popping and pounding, but from having to go back to our normal lives. Without a doubt, I was in love with my best friend. God, how can this be if it's so hard? If we have to go through all these things, is it really meant to be? God didn't seem to answer me, so I was left with questions echoing in my head.

It was back to the grind, back to being just friends with no physical contact. It wasn't hard, more like excruciating. We went on dates, our version of dates anyway, with a minimum of a foot apart, so we looked like just friends. We didn't get too close, but we had to be so careful. We didn't hold hands, he could never put his arm around me, and we had to be a little bit at a distance. It was hard, but we spent a lot of those cold Alaska nights snuggled up, holding hands, or with our legs touching each other on the couch, kissing of course (blush).

One night, we went out to dinner at one of the local favorites, Lavelle's.

"This isn't fair," I protested. "I don't like having to be secret. I want to hold hands with you. I love you!"

He placed his hands over mine for twenty seconds of pure happiness. Fox came in the door, and we quickly separated our hands.

"That was close," I said to Stephen. "Do you think he saw?"

"No. He would have said something."

The next day, a high-ranking sergeant in our unit, Sergeant First Class Javelin, called us into his office. I thought maybe he was just giving us some information because he was in charge of S-1 section, which took care of administrative and logistic matters. He called us both into the office and motioned for us to sit in the chairs.

He closed the door. "Now, you guys know I like you," he began. "I think you're both good people and good soldiers, but I saw you guys last night. Now, off the record, I don't care what you guys do on your personal time, but, on the record, don't be stupid about it. You know that's not going to fly with Chaplain Eagle. I don't want any part of this, so just do me a favor, and don't be holding hands in public. Whatever you do behind closed doors is your business, but when you do it in public, it makes it everyone's business, so consider this a warning."

He motioned for us to get up and leave. In unison, we snapped to parade rest, "Yes, Sergeant." We were dismissed. So Fox hadn't seen us, but Sergeant Javelin had! What should we do? We weren't going to dissolve our relationship—we loved each other. I couldn't blame Sergeant Javelin. He didn't want to fight a battle that wasn't his to fight. He probably had his family to think about. He didn't know the whole story, that we were dating beforehand, and we didn't divulge that information.

I see that God's favor was with us through it all. Had this been another sergeant in our unit, or Eagle himself, things would have gone down differently. Sure, we had been reprimanded, but I knew where I was coming from. Sergeant Javelin was a good leader who genuinely cared about his soldiers, but I believe he knew what was going on in the background. I believe he knew about Chaplain Eagle's character. He knew that Article 15, along with other punishable actions, would have been enforced had it been Chaplain Eagle. Sergeant Javelin was looking out for us. Had we not had time to build our relationship, it would not have been anywhere near strong enough for the things that were to come.

Chapter 15

Sleeping Arrangements

One night, I woke up, startled in the middle of the night, and saw my curtain swaying a bit, as if someone had just been there. It's probably just my roommate Paisley. I shouldn't have drunk all that water before bed; now I was awake, and I had to pee something fierce. As I pushed back the curtain that separated my space from my roommate's, I gasped and nearly jumped out of my skin. Paisley's boyfriend was silently leaned up against the wall. What was he doing there? I had this eerie feeling that spooked me awake, and then it looked as if he was looming around.

"Sorry. Didn't mean to scare you."

Wait… was he staring at me in my sleep? The hair on the back of my neck stood up, and I shuddered. I had no lock for my side of the room because I didn't even have a door. The influx of soldiers into Alaska meant that I had to double up with a roommate. Our barracks were turned into Army lodging. What that meant for roommates was that one person had the bedroom with the door, while the other had the living

Sleeping Arrangements

room side, which housed a mini-fridge and microwave. Instead of the couch, the unit had issued me a twin-sized bed. I was okay with Paisley coming onto my side of the room because, I reasoned, the fridge and microwave were in my area. We shared a bathroom, which was in the middle of our room, that was constantly messy.

I am notorious for flinging my clothes on my bed, as I decide what to wear. They might miss the bed and end up on the floor, but my roommate brought it to the next level. I had to clean up after Paisley every time before I used the bathroom. There were dirty clothes, toothpaste all over the sink, and the sink looked as if it hadn't been cleaned in weeks, even though I consistently cleaned it. She left food out constantly, and there were crusty bowls on our bathroom counter from cereal or remnants of leftovers. The worst was when she forgot about the broccoli in the fridge, and the room, especially my side where the fridge was and where the garbage was, stunk horribly. I got used to having her as a roommate. Despite her flaws, she was a sweetheart and was always kind to me. What I was not prepared for was my roommate's new boyfriend. She had asked me prior to that night about him staying over.

"Hey. Do you mind if my boyfriend stays over?"

"No, that's fine."

I figured it would be. He was coming over to stay on her side, after all, so it wasn't a big deal. As days went on, I came home often to him being there without her. No big deal. She probably gave him her key, and she will be here soon, I rationalized. In the following weeks, I realized my roommate was leaving the key under our welcome mat, a most obvious place, so he could get into our room before she was there. I had only been her roommate for just under a month, and he started to stay over most nights. I decided I needed a curtain rod with a curtain, so I could at least get dressed on my side and have some privacy. Paisley's boyfriend barged in, just as she did, on my side to use the fridge. While I was annoyed but okay with my roommate doing that, being that I knew her and we were both girls, I was not okay with him doing that. I asked if they could knock on the wall to make sure I was fully dressed before they walked in. Eventually, I moved our fridge, with the microwave on top, to right outside my curtain to the left of the bathroom so that no one needed to traipse through my side of the room, whether or not I was there.

The rules of the barracks were the same as when I snuck my sister in—there were to be no sleepovers. I wasn't going to be a narc.

Time went on, and things got stranger. I woke up in the middle of the night with the feeling that someone had just been in my room. Every time I opened my curtain, I saw him lurking in the middle space, outside of the bathroom. Why couldn't he just be on her side? She wasn't always there, but it seemed to me as if he was always there.

I started to experience extreme anxiety because of the time my curtain moved when I was awake. I wasn't sure my "roomie" would believe that her boyfriend was a creeper, and I didn't really have proof. Maybe I was just paranoid? I started spending all my waking hours with Stephen in his room, and that lessened the number of encounters. I felt uncomfortable in my room. I couldn't feel comfortable, even in my most comfy, soft pajamas. After a few weeks of sleepless nights, I told Stephen I didn't feel safe there.

Stephen was understanding and also disturbed that the boyfriend was behaving this way, but I made him promise not to say anything to Paisley because I didn't want it to be a tense situation. I had all my clothes and stuff in my room still, but with Stephen allowing me to spend the night in his room almost every night, it started being just when Paisley's boyfriend was there. I bought an extra toothbrush and toiletries that I left in Stephen's bathroom. Let's not pretend here—I was excited to "live" with Stephen, even though I knew my parents would not approve of this cohabitation without marriage. I knew I shouldn't, but I knew I was in love with my boyfriend. He was kind, and he was safe.

The tricky part was how to get to his room. Our supervisor was diagonally across the hall from Stephen, as well as a few people from our company who were on either side of his room. They were on the first floor. My room was on the second. I went downstairs into the creepy fluorescent blinking lights, into the basement where the laundry room and storage were, and back up the stairs, so I didn't have to walk by our supervisor's door. I called Stephen to make sure the coast was clear and snuck in that way.

One night, Sergeant Church knocked on the door while I was getting ready for bed. I shuffled into the bedroom and dove behind the couch.

"Hayes, I'm just checking for Whiteman. She didn't answer her door, and I wanted to tell her something for tomorrow." We had had several close calls, so I knew to jump into the closet, behind the bed, or on the side of the couch near the kitchen, but it was best to go into the bedroom, in case Sergeant Church came into Stephen's room.

There were a few times I almost got caught on my way to Stephen's room to spend the night but then I just went back to my room, as if I had laundry or was just knocking on someone else's door. We kept this up for a good year. I don't know if Sergeant Church actually knew what was going on, but as long as we didn't get caught, I think he just decided to look the other way. Looking back on it, maybe that makes more sense. He might have decided it was none of his business what Stephen was doing in his spare time. Or maybe I was just full of soldier stealth.

CAMOUFLAGED LOVE

Chapter 16

Intel

One particular instance can change your trajectory or could ruin your life. Thankfully, all my missteps have not had lasting ramifications, and thank God for that. I wasn't into drinking, and the two separate times I did drink in the Army, it was in excess, and it ended miserably with a hangover.

Once was accidentally, as I lost a drinking card game, and once was right after my breakup with Cypress. I had gone to another soldier's hangout on a Saturday night, and they were mixing all types of alcohol, and I ended the night puking out my intestines. Sergeant Church sent me home that time from work. I had chapel duty that particular Sunday, and he was also on duty. I had a pounding headache. He could tell I had had a rough Saturday night.

"I can tell you have a hangover. Don't do that ever again. It's just a warning this time. Make smart choices." That was a moment of grace that I was grateful for.

On my twenty-first birthday, some of my friends and I went to Chili's. It was one of the only chain restaurants in Fairbanks that was open later. I ate chicken tenders and fries and decided I wanted to try a fruity drink. I took one sip, and it was too strong, so I gave it to my friend. I ordered another drink and took a sip but didn't want to finish it. It was too sour for my liking. Stephen was not into the club scene, but he agreed to come along because he knew I wanted to go out. We went to "the club," which was really more of a bar with a small, cracked-tiled, cube-shaped dance floor, set in the middle of nowhere in North Pole, Alaska. I was freezing waiting for them to open the doors, as it was negative forty degrees that night, and I dressed up in my denim miniskirt, with my red top and matching red heels, and my puffy blue jacket. Stephen gave me his jacket while waiting in line, after sighing and, with his most practical nature, thinking that he tried to tell me I was going to be cold.

While I tried the different drinks at the bar, other soldiers I knew from various units were at the bar. They found out it was my birthday and bought me a drink. I drank a little of every drink that I had been given, but there were about ten different drinks in total that I tried. After King tried to give me another drink, Stephen said, "I think she's had enough." We danced on the dance floor, which was uneven. I was having fun and being carefree, but little did I know that my friend was watching me, as I was drinking, and Stephen was watching him. I was not drunk, but I definitely felt the effects of the alcohol. King had finished all the drinks I had not. Suddenly, there was a lot of yelling, and a woman almost knocked me over as she brushed past me, looking for her coat that someone had stolen. A fight was on the verge of breaking out.

I almost fell, but Stephen caught my elbow and arm and steadied me.

He said to King, "It's time to go."

Intel

Stephen drove my friend's truck home, as King had been drinking as well. After we returned to our barracks, King came inside my room, along with Stephen.

"Are you two dating?" King asked. I had not told all of my Alaskan friends we were dating because of our supervisors. I tried to avoid the question. He looked at me.

"I would date you if I could," he said. I laughed, thinking he was joking.

He looked down at the floor and frowned. I hadn't seen my friend date anyone, but I did not seem him in that light.

"Yes. We're dating."

King worked as a paralegal in the JAG office, and after that day, we still were friends, but I didn't see him as much.

As the weeks and months went by, I grew closer to fellow chaplain assistants from the brigade, as the time came for the Army brigade to deploy. Some of them came to help me take care of the lawn maintenance or help deep clean the chapel. Some invited Stephen and me to a meal at their houses, or they invited us to spend time together. They took care of their units and checked on me, in the midst of not fully knowing what Stephen and I were facing.

Typically, you need a certain time spent in a rank or current position in order to move up in the Army ranking system, and it was usually a year. Special consideration could be applied sooner than the normal waiting period to get promoted, but a soldier had to stand out among peers. Doing the minimum wouldn't cut it. A soldier must go above and beyond in professional performance.

After cleaning the chapel following an event, Stephen turned to me.

"You have been doing a lot, especially before I got here. You were running three different areas of operation. I'm sure you can get promoted early."

Stephen helped me gather the documentation of all the events and services I had been managing. Stephen encouraged me and guided me to get submitted for a promotion to specialist, he helped me showcase all the things I was doing to prove that I had been working above my rank, and holding down our section while everyone else was in their school.

We also thought it couldn't hurt, as it made it even harder for Chaplain Eagle to say two specialists couldn't date. He printed the recommendation and printed it, and my chaplain signed it. Chaplain Sword also helped me by allowing me to take classes and supporting me. Most times, my chaplain was able to run interference so that Chaplain Eagle wasn't always able to have full access to me, as I had to help my chaplain at our building, be there when he was counseling people at the front desk, and be present when he was counseling someone of the opposite sex.

Stephen submitted the form to Sergeant Church, and then to the admin office, for processing. It was about a month or so before I was told I would be promoted.

I wanted to celebrate my promotion, so the day after my promotion, I decided I wanted to do something fun to celebrate. I invited Jessica, Chaplain Eagle's daughter, to come with me to play laser tag with Stephen and me. She came to my barracks room as I got ready for our fun, and I filled her in on last week's car troubles and how Stephen had helped me.

Intel

"Aww… You know, Lorin, I can tell by the way you look when you talk about him that you like him."

I froze. *Uh oh. If Chaplain Eagle's daughter knows…*

"How will your family feel about that? I know my dad would not be okay with that. I could be friends, but to bring a boyfriend home who was black wouldn't fly. He thinks people should be with people who look the same." My heart sank.

I just couldn't understand. How could anyone, especially a chaplain, one who cares about people, not love a person who cares about others? How could someone harbor hate in their heart for anyone, especially Stephen? When I thought about how Chaplain Eagle preached about love on Sundays, teaching about how God wants us to work together, my stomach churned. I just couldn't understand. In the chaplain corps, made up of chaplains and chaplain assistants, we were responsible for the morale. We were held to a higher standard. Not that chaplain assistants or chaplains never cursed or did bad things, but in the military world where profanity is commonplace, we were supposed to be different in our words and actions. Some of the soldiers I knew who weren't Christians weren't hateful, yet here was a chaplain who was supposed to be a model of God, the Father's, love, and who was supposed to lead others into God's word… wasn't he?

As a Christian, my core belief is that God is love, that the two greatest commandments are to love God and love others. Well, I wasn't feeling the love.

Chapter 17

The Exodus

"When will you marry me?"

I poked Stephen. We had been secretly dating for over a year.

"I know you said you will, but are you sure you are ready to meet all the crazy? My father's side is loud, and my mother's side is loud. And opinionated. And loving. Did I mention a side of crazy?"

My mom had talked to Stephen on the phone before, and I had talked endlessly about him. My family teased me because the previous December, after knowing him for maybe two months, we went our separate ways on Christmas leave (vacation), and I still spent a good chunk of time on the phone with him. December was only a month away. I knew that we wouldn't be able to take Christmas leave during December since we did the previous year, but January could work.

I wanted my family to meet my man. I wanted to show him

The Exodus

where I came from. How his Texas soul was oh so wrong, that all pizza is not created equal, that it isn't just pizza. We New Yorkers take our pizza very seriously.

The first time we ordered pizza together may have been our first argument.

"This isn't good," I said.

"It's just pizza. Pizza is pizza."

"Um... excuse me. Pizza is not created equal!" I puffed up my chest. "New York pizza is the best pizza, and it's not like this fast food pizza. It is not the same."

Stephen raised his eyebrow. "It's just pizza," he repeated.

I smiled smugly. "You don't know any better, but when you visit my family, you will see."

We had debated and been back and forth. I am the absolute worst at deceit, but I thought we should fudge our leave location from the record. For accountability purposes, they wanted to see an itinerary for days flying in and out. The Army must know the whereabouts of your leave (vacation time) and the exact dates for coverage of your unit.

So, here we were, debating what to do.

"They will never approve our leave if they see that we are going together. Why don't we leave out the part that we will be together for a week," I suggested. The plan was for him to come to New York with me for a week, then go to Texas for a week.

"What if we have you go to Texas and then New York the same day?" I suggested.

"No." Stephen was tired, tired of the BS, tired of the running around, and tired of jumping through hoops. "We are serious, and we are going to get married anyway, so I don't care. And if we make up the dates, then we could get into trouble for lying to an officer and NCO." I felt overwhelmed with love for him. He loved me and wanted to let the world know. Unlike Cypress, he wanted to shout from the rooftops that he was proud of me and he loved me!

He not only attached his leave to his form, but mine as well, and he brazenly handed them in, complete with the coinciding dates, to Sergeant Church. Immediately, we were called into his office. "What are you guys doing? What are you thinking? You should have just done this without sending in your itinerary."

After being released at the end-of-day formation, Sergeant Church called Stephen and me to the side.

"Chaplain is trying to figure out how to write you an Article 15 for fraternization. You guys could have avoided this whole thing by not telling on yourselves. Now he is threatening to cancel your leave, give extra duty, give an Article 15. This is stupid." An Article 15 can come with a demotion, loss of pay, and a negative record that could potentially lead to the Army kicking you out.

Yes. Why, yes it is stupid! "Sergeant, whether or not we visit one another's families, we are getting married, and no amount of pushback is going to stop us. We love each other. Why can't you guys be happy for us?"

He replied, "He just worries if things don't work out between you, how is it going to look? How will you guys work together after you

The Exodus

break up? The morale of the whole unit will be down. He doesn't want your relationship to interfere with getting your job done." I didn't completely understand. He thought Stephen was a good worker and person, and he seemed okay with him, until it came to us dating. Stephen said he had a sneaking suspicion he knew why Chaplain Eagle had such a hard time with us being together. I didn't understand. It didn't make sense to me. Chaplain Eagle was in charge of all the chaplains and chaplain assistants, and there were people of different ethnicities—white, black, Asian, Latino. He never outwardly did or said anything that led me to believe it was because of Stephen's skin color, but surely there was another explanation. Maybe it really was that they didn't want us dating because they really thought it would ruin the camaraderie if we didn't work out?

After an anguishing four days went by, we were once again at parade rest in front of Sergeant Church. "Chaplain Eagle has decided that he will let you guys go on leave, but there will be further discussions when you get back. You are to tell no one. Understood?" Understood? What I understood was my family was going to finally meet the man of my dreams, and I was going to meet his! I was baffled but I nodded. I anxiously counted down the days.

Sergeant Church was on board with Chaplain Eagle because why else wouldn't he stand up for us? Why wouldn't he help Chaplain Eagle see that we were still good workers, and he could just reassign one of us to the other chapel?

Our supervisor could come back and cancel our leave at any time. I didn't know what was going to happen. I teetered between confidence that God would make it work out and great anxiety. I kept praying. God, please work this out for us. You know my heart. You know I love Stephen, but if it's this hard, is it supposed to be? If it's your will, shouldn't things pan out and go relatively smoothly, if it's meant to be? I felt waves of peace, even when my worry seemed determined to choke out my happiness.

I worried that they were going to cancel our leave up until we were seated side by side on the plane, and as our plane took off, I said a prayer of gratitude.

Chapter 18

New York State of Mind

Stephen's welcome to the concrete jungle was, unfortunately, the terror of a taxi ride. Our taxi driver had to be the epitome of whatever others perceive of a New York taxi driver. Dangerous to those on the road, flying around, swerving, slamming on the breaks, all while trying to navigate and text someone on his phone, it was straight out of a sitcom. Stephen's jaw locked up, and he looked a little green. Stephen leaned forward and said, "Hey! You are going into the other lane. Do you need me to help you so we get there safely?"

My stomach felt a bit queasy as well. I squeezed Stephen's hand so I didn't yell at the last-minute stops and close calls of nearly sideswiping a vehicle. I prayed to God that we would make it in one piece and imagined what kind of tragic story would be in tomorrow's paper if this was, indeed, the end. It would say something like, "Love birds met tragedy on the way to meet family," or, "Two Alaskan soldiers join the ranks of those gone before."

"New York drivers are crazy!" Stephen muttered.

I wanted to say not all New York drivers, but it seemed futile.

"Well, I guess the stereotype comes from some truth."

Thankfully, God allowed us to get to my grandma's house. We arrived, shaken up, but fully alive and well. The snow was cleared off the road but still piled up on the side. Unlike Alaska, it was above freezing. I had only ever seen maybe negative twenty degrees with the wind chill in New York. It felt hot to us, coming from negative fifty degrees to the thirties.

We knocked on the door, and my grandma Diane moved as swift as her four-foot ten-inch body could move her. She cried happy tears, yelled with excitement, and hugged and kissed us on both cheeks, then said, "I am so happy you are here. You must be hungry. I made gravy and spaghetti."

Yum! My grandmother is Italian, and there is nothing like her sauce. Some Italian-Americans call sauce gravy, so whatever you want to call it, it was delish. The secret to her sauce is the amount of time it takes to simmer, a minimum of six hours. She made her sauce with meatballs, sausage, and love. Stephen enjoyed the food, since Italian was his favorite (God's bonus in me). My mom had driven down to meet us at Grandma's house with my sister and some of my cousins from her side. We all just chatted, and they got to know how funny and how charming my love was. Stephen flashed his smile and laughed his comic-book laugh, the kind of laugh that you can see written out in words. It's one of the things I love about him, and it's contagious. We got to stretch our legs and relax for a few hours before the next stop on our journey.

We drove into Brooklyn to my Uncle Tommy's house where my Uncle Jimmy and his son, my cousin Tommy, were waiting for us. They had ordered us the best pizza ever as far, as I'm concerned (Disclaimer: I've yet to go to the motherland.), Brooklyn Pizza. Stephen's poor soul tried to tell me in Alaska that pizza is just pizza. Pizza is not created equal, and after one bite of the perfectly baked brick oven pizza, as the gooey cheese that became perfectly cooked sauce shocked his taste buds, he understood why I'm a bit of a pizza snob. One bite of an authentic Brooklyn pizzeria pizza, and he took back his blasphemy.

"Mmmm," was all he said, as he stuffed his face. "Wow! This is the best pizza I've ever had!"

"Told you…" I smiled triumphantly.

Afterward, we went to Staten Island, to my Aunt Dee's house, to stay for the night. We had planned a trip into the city (Manhattan) to show him all the favorite tourist spots. Meeting up with my cousins in Staten Island was preplanned. We planned all the things people typically do when they visit the city, what makes New York so special, like taking the train to the subway. We took the ferry around the Statue of Liberty. We went to Rockefeller Center. We ate lunch at the Hard Rock Cafe. We then adventured into the enormous four- story FAO Schwartz. Stephen, Lianne, and I had a giant Pixy Stix sword fight. Hey, everyone is a kid at heart, and who wouldn't want to visit the largest toy store in the world?

We traveled by subway, and I think that made Stephen a bit squeamish. There were a lot of people, and he likes his space, and he's a bit of a germophobe. We got to listen to the musical prowess of the people of New York, quartet style, playing on the corner. We had a good time walking around, except for the one guy who kept hustling, trying to push a CD on my sixteen-year-old sister. He insisted she take his new CD, and her gentle spirit, after saying no, had her reluctantly taking it as he shoved it into her hands. Promptly, he heckled her for the money to pay for it. My cousin, Nicole, got into it with him. "Don't touch her! Take back this CD, and get the hell out of here!" Stephen stepped in beside her, as the guy got toe to toe with my cousin. My cousin could hold her own, but Stephen has always been a protector of people and can get serious when he needs to. People were always hustling on the corners in the city, and my cousin was certainly more used to it than I was. We visited my family in the city at least once a month, and they lived down there. Stephen, with his sweet Southern heart, tried to say hello every time he made eye contact with someone on the sidewalk.

"I love that you are such a southern gentleman, but you can't do that here. First off, we don't want to look 'touristy,' and second, you literally cannot say hello to everyone you see. There are too many people."

That advice may have fallen on deaf ears. He couldn't help himself. Bless his heart.

"When I make eye contact, I'm going to say hello because that's what I was taught." I did try to tell him beforehand, but I think he was overwhelmed by the sheer number of people. He was from Texas, from Dallas, so I thought he would be fine.

We showed Stephen around and then visited Central Park, and he got to see the people of New York—well, some of the performers who dressed up like statues or the workers who rushed by, late to

New York State of Mind

their next appointment. There is an air of busyness, as well as smog, in New York City, but there are good humans there too. Not everyone is heartless and rude as portrayed in every movie and TV series, but, yes, it's a bit of a picture of the hustle and bustle of people on a mission. I had always told Stephen he couldn't show the same hospitality as in the south. It's impractical to say hello to everyone you see pass you on the sidewalk. There are far too many people. There are nice people, but there are rude people, just like anywhere, but there are millions of people. The more people, the more crowded, and the more aggravated you get when you can't get to where you want to quickly.

We also went to where the twin towers used to be, and the memorial stood in its place. It was very emotional for me, as I remembered the events of 9/11 and the weeks that followed. I remembered the dust cloud that stretched to my aunt's house in Staten Island for weeks afterward, and I remembered my grandfather who was an inspector and was on the ground during the cleanup and aftermath. I put a flower in the fence, along with many other cards and flowers, and I cried while Stephen held me. We finished the day exhausted, feet sore, and we took the train back to my aunt's.

We then made the two-and-a-half-hour trek to upstate New York with my mom and sister. As my mom's car climbed the winding roads that became more and more rural, Stephen fidgeted with his hands and bounced his leg. I took his hand in mine and whispered in his ear, "My dad is going to love you. Don't worry!"

"It's not that. I'm just feeling anxious. This reminds me of some country places I have been before. Let's just say they didn't like me being around."

Any time that he had been in a rural place, it had not meant good news for him. He had been chased out of towns, not so much with specific words like people saying, "You're not welcome here." Instead, he had been told by a shotgun wielding store owner that a gas station was closed, even though it was obviously open, evident from the sign and additional people in the store. He had been asked, "You lost, boy?" as he travelled through states with his mom and sister as a kid and as a teenager, so he was anxious as the rural environment reminded him of those encounters.

I thought maybe he was also a little nervous about meeting my dad, too, even if he didn't say so.

I squeezed his hand.

"You're going to be okay. My dad is going to love you, and everyone who meets you is going to love you!"

My dad is a kind guy. He is always joking, and he is always helping other people, but he still has a little bit of Brooklyn in him, and I was his firstborn. My first boyfriend had the first experience with my dad. My first boyfriend had told us that a lot can be learned about a person by studying their handwriting. My dad gave him a paper with his name and some writing on it. "Okay. Decode this." He slipped him a paper that was supposed to have his name on it. It read, "John, if you hurt my daughter, I'll kill you." Needless to say, my first boyfriend was petrified. Another time, my father was cleaning his gun when a perspective admirer came around, or there was the time that my "Poppy" brought out his baseball bat upon meeting that same guy, saying, "This is called Brooklyn justice." Can we please just put the threats and weapons away?

However, my dad is a good judge of character. He never threatened or cleaned his gun in front of Stephen. He did, however, take him on a drive with him to get to know him and talk to him. Stephen never said what exactly the conversation entailed, but my dad and he attest to the fact that there were no threats made. We spent several days meeting my friends, including my best friend, Savannah, hanging out at my parent's house, and just relaxing. We made some piña coladas, which have always been my favorite when they are made from cream of coconut, homemade style, and we sang karaoke with my family.

I was sure my parents would be fine with me dating a black guy, and they were. As long as they treated me right, my parents had never cared what my friends or prospective beaux looked like. But what about my extended family? I remember one year, after getting tired of waiting on a teenager hand and foot, a family member said, "What? Do I look a shade darker to you?" I almost spit out my drink. Sometimes people don't even realize what they say or the implications of what they say.

Two days before Stephen had to leave to go to Texas to see his family, we had one last family get together at my Uncle Richie and Aunt Kathy's house in Jersey, so everyone who hadn't seen and met Stephen yet would get the chance. I was having a blast. We were playing Gestures and Taboo, and there was once again delicious food, including lasagna, Italian flag cookies—or as I call them, rainbow cookies—bruschetta, and the whole spread, which is typical in my family. It's like a five-course meal—so much food! Stephen disappeared upstairs, and I thought he was playing a video game with my sister and my cousin, Anthony. Stephen had been sweating and was acting funny, so he told my sister what he was planning to do.

"I've been carrying around a small black box in my pocket," he divulged to her.

My sister became his hype man, saying, "You can do this!"

Stephen paced back and forth nervously.

My Aunt Lisa tried to gather everyone to say the blessing and to eat dinner. Stephen said he would help, and he took this as the perfect opportunity. "Hey! Hey! Everyone come to the dining table. It's time for food." As soon as everyone was gathered, he started, "I just wanted to say thank you everyone. Everyone has been so hospitable, and I needed to get everyone to hear me." He locked eyes with me. "The real reason I wanted everyone to gather here is because I have an important announcement."

He got down on his knee. I screamed in my head with excitement.

"I love you, Lorin, and I want to spend the rest of my life with you, showing you everyday how much I love you. You are the love of my life, and I feel God brought me all the way to Alaska because I had to find you. Will you do the honor of being my wife? Will you marry me?"

"Yes! Yes!" I hugged him. He tried to put the ring on my finger, but I was shaking like a leaf, and he was also shaking too much. I had to help him and then I hugged him before he was able to get off the floor.

My family celebrated and popped some champagne. I was surprised and never saw it coming. This was a good surprise. My aunt and uncle still talk about it to this day about what an honor it was to have that happen at their house. Some people might want a proposal at a fancy restaurant, but he knew that to me, family is everything. He had asked my dad for a blessing on that car ride, asked to propose, and he got it. I always asked Stephen what he would have done if my dad had said no.

"I would have worked on our relationship until he was okay with it."

New York State of Mind

He knew my dad was a good man, and my family meant a lot to me. He would have honored and trusted my dad's judgment and waited for me.

After all the pictures, hugs, and the Italian kisses on both cheeks (mwah, mwah), the chatter settled done. My family started asking when we were going to get married. Stephen and I had already discussed, in Alaska, the plan to get married, and we talked about a short engagement of maybe six months, so I told them it would probably be June.

"Wait! Are you pregnant?" My dad's forehead wrinkled with concern.

"No, Dad! What in the world?!?"

"Hey. I'm just checking because that is a pretty short engagement, and I want to make sure you guys are getting married for the right reasons."

No, there were no babies on the horizon. We didn't want Chaplain Eagle to use his influence to send us to different ends of the world to separate us. We didn't want the Army to send one of us to another duty station if we came up on orders. As soon as possible, we needed to get our paperwork done, so there was a better chance the Army would try to keep us stationed together.

Chapter 19

She's White

In November, I had joined the local on-post basketball team with Stephen and Fox. I was the only female on our team, and our unit was so small that they drafted the three of us to another unit team. We went to the gym on Saturdays to play pick-up games, mostly so we could improve our game, and so I could gain some confidence. For one of our first games, the gym was nearly empty, except for a few soldiers speckled here and there in the bleachers, along with some people's significant others.

One girl decided to sit so close to our stuff that I had to reach between her legs to reach my stuff. I rolled my eyes, as I reached for my things. Why are you standing on my jacket and that close to my things!

"Excuse me… I don't mean to be all up in your grill."

I used to say this phrase all the time, but I said it sarcastically because she gave me a look as if I was in the wrong. The girl, who happened to be Stephen's complexion, balled her fists and gave me an incredulous look, then looked up at Stephen.

Stephen came over, apologizing for me, trying to diffuse the situation.

"She doesn't realize what she's saying. So sorry." I clicked my teeth.

"Um… yes I know what I'm saying, and she's literally on top of my stuff and giving me a look like I'm crazy for being in her space," I defended.

Stephen stepped between us and led me away peacefully.

"I didn't say anything wrong, and I'm not sorry." We made our way to the car.

I hissed at him, "Don't apologize for me. I can apologize when I need to. I wasn't sorry!"

"To an outsider, it looked like you were mocking her because she was black, and you were trying to use Ebonics."

"I always say that, though. You hear me say 'up in your grill' all the time."

Stephen nodded. "Yes, but she doesn't know that. It looked like you were making fun of her."

My words seemed to be mocking her, and to him, her reaction to our exchange appeared as if she wanted to fight me. But, I didn't do anything! However, clearly that was lost in translation. The appearance of something, with its intent being missed, can lead people to receive things in different ways. I meant no harm with my words, but I didn't know her experiences with white people. I didn't know whether she had been belittled, jested at using Ebonics, or made to feel some other negative way.

It occurred to me just a few years ago how some phrases in society are said without thinking twice. Two phrases I know I have heard are, "Wait one cotton-picking minute," and, "Wow! You're a slave driver."

Even though it made me uncomfortable at times, I didn't even think about how that could deeply wound someone or make them feel, when it was something that was linked to their ancestors. I always took it for granted. I thought, for that first phrase, maybe it took forever to pick cotton. At that stage of my life, it had a different connotation to me. If someone said that to someone of color, I believed that to be very hurtful, degrading because of slavery, for the ones who picked the cotton. Or imagine calling someone of color a "slave driver," someone whose ancestors were actually enslaved. What kind of emotions would that draw up? I imagined how Stephen's older relatives would have felt hearing that phrase, "Wait one cotton-picking minute," as some in the older generation had, in real life, worked picking cotton. We aren't that far removed from slavery and all its cotton picking. It's hurtful, inconsiderate at best, and downright hateful, with racist undertones at their worst. This was systemic racism, phrases and meanings that so flippant that the implications can be incredibly harmful. It's easy to push aside if we have no ties to it, if it doesn't affect us directly. Some argue that others are too sensitive. I would argue we are not sensitive enough to the plight of other people's hardships. We need to do better to practice some awareness and some empathy.

Not only were Stephen and I ebony and ivory, but we were

She's White

from two different worlds, the north and the south, New York and Texas. I remember one time, we had this whole argument while trying to buy a pizza.

"Just order a cheese pie." In New York this is understood to mean a pizza pie. In Stephen's world, deep in the heart of Texas, a pie is a baked dessert. He was familiar with pecan, apple, or sweet potato pies, but he was disgusted by my mention of a cheese pie.

Finally, exasperated, he told me, "That doesn't even sound good. We're trying to order pizza here."

"Yes, I know we are ordering pizza. A cheese pie is another name for pizza!"

Miscommunication happens all the time, but when you have a different view or different experiences, things are interpreted differently. Is Stephen's family going to accept me? It had gone so well with my family. I thought it was too good to be true. What are the chances that they will accept me, just as my family accepted him? What if I said something insensitive, like the "up in your grill" thing?

Stephen picked me up from the airport, and I ran and jumped on him, smothering him with kisses. He put my suitcase in the back of the rental, and we were off to meet his mom first. We were staying at her apartment. I bit my lip, as I looked out the window.

Stephen's mom was in the Army, like us. At least that could be a talking point. She was in the National Guard, and she was a few hours away from the rest of the family. We arrived, and my hands felt clammy as Stephen knocked on the door.

"Ah! It's so good to see you!"

She hugged her son tight, and for a moment, I wasn't sure what to do, so I just stood there waiting. She turned toward me and enveloped me in a hug.

"Hi! It's nice to meet you. Come in. You must be tired from all that traveling."

In person, she was just as warm and charismatic as she had been over the phone. As she showed us around her apartment, I looked at all the pictures on the wall. I love pictures and tried to see all of Stephen's family to gather any intel I could in order to connect with them and to know who was who. My eyes locked on one particular picture, and I felt the color drain from my face. On the wall hung a picture of Stephen next to a woman in a matching yellow warmup suit. This obviously was a previous relationship. I excused myself because I was upset. She still wanted them together. Why else would she have that picture? Was it because I was white? Stephen realized what had happened and asked his mom if she would take down the picture. She didn't apologize for the picture as she showed off the wall (I think she was embarrassed and hoped I hadn't seen that particular one), so she never pointed it out. I assumed she liked that girl better and that she pined for them to mend their relationship. Stephen assured me it wasn't the case, and his mom apologized for the picture, saying it was the most recent picture she had of Stephen as an adult, so we needed to send her one for her to put up instead. We had a nice evening talking, and Stephen caught his mom up on events. We were planning on driving to Louisiana in the morning to watch his sister's college basketball game and visit.

Brenita was Stephen's younger sister. She was in college and a star athlete on her team. She ran like a gazelle on the court, as she scored basket after basket. Beyond her obvious skills, it was apparent

She's White

that she played with her heart and had passion for the sport. I was nervous to meet her because I know how much I respect and care about my own sister's impression.

After they won their game, she signed a few team posters and shirts for their supporters and fans. As soon as she saw Stephen, she rushed to jump and hug Stephen. I love seeing siblings together. I saw the mutual love and respect for each other, as they both had tears in their eyes. I knew Stephen was proud of her, and I sensed she was proud of her big brother, too. Luckily, she was kind, and we hit it off pretty quickly. I teased Stephen because I found out his sister and I were the same age as each other.

As we walked outside and down the steps of the gym, we were greeted by her boyfriend. I thought they were a cute couple, and I kept nudging big brother Stephen to loosen up as he gave him the third degree. Stephen shook his hand firmly at the introduction, "And what are your intentions with my sister?" Wow… he cuts right to the chase, doesn't he?

Stephen's sister was hilarious and sweet, someone whom I would befriend for myself, whether or not I was dating her brother. I was enamored with Stephen, and I think she could tell, so besides asking me questions to get to know me, she didn't give me a hard time. We went out to dinner, then we brought her back to her dorm room off campus. After a tour of her apartment, we had to get back on the road. It was a tearful goodbye. Stephen and Brenita hugged, and it made me miss my sister. I reflected on how hard it was to be away from siblings when we were stationed so far away.

The next day, we left to visit Stephen's grandmother's house. I gathered from stories that Grandmother was the matriarch of the family, and her house was the hub of all things, all family functions, and all gatherings. This was a big deal. They were having a barbecue for Stephen and specifically invited everyone to meet me and see him. Even though I seemed to pass the test with his mom and sister, I knew how much his entire family meant to him. I wasn't sure if everyone would approve. I nervously jiggled my leg for the last twenty minutes of the trip.

I tried to control my breathing, and when he opened my door for me, Stephen took notice.

"They are going to love you. Don't worry. Are you ready?" I took in a deep breath and nodded. Get a grip on yourself. We came to the entryway of a single-story red, brick house. Stephen knocked and then opened the door, entering the dim hallway to the green carpeted living room. I trailed behind him.

"Everyone, I want you to meet my fiancée, Lorin." I stepped out of the shadows and waved nervously, smiling and pushing my hair out of my face.

"SHE'S WHITE?!?" spoke the raspier voice of his one of his aunts. It was like a record scratch. All speaking ceased abruptly, and people whipped their heads toward me. My heart pounded in my chest, and my face flushed. I sucked my lips in, and my knees wobbled. Time seemed to stand still. You could cut the tension with a knife. Stephen broke through the thick air, "Yes. Yes, she is."

Then another voice interjected, "Well, could you blame him, after that last one?"

She's White

"True…"

"Well, okay then!" said warmly the raspier voice.

People cracked up and started coming near us to greet us. They welcomed me with arms outstretched. They asked me where my daughter was. I didn't have any kids! Some family members had seen a picture of me, but obviously not all of them! Stephen didn't have many pictures of me because I was self-conscious, so the only one he had was one he had taken from me—of my baby cousin and me. That made me feel better because they were ready to welcome me, even with a baby they had believed was mine.

The day before we left to go back to Alaska, we did one more thing as a family. A number of family members—aunts, cousins, his mom, and sister—took us to the movies. We were in the concession line being waited on, still deciding on snacks. I considered gummy bears, and Stephen's mom tried to decide what to get besides popcorn.

Another concession stand worker said, "Can I help who is next?"

No one answered. "I said, can I help who's next?!?" I looked around, but I didn't see anyone else in line. I was standing to the side, slightly behind Stephen.

"You! You, right there!" She pointed straight at me, as I looked left and right I pointed to myself. I was about to tell her I was with them, but she whipped her neck so hard I thought it might break.

"I said, can I help who is next. You are next."

Stephen said, "Wow, that's embarrassing. She's with us! We are all together."

She was mortified. She didn't say another word, but ducked

behind the counter and disappeared. She didn't apologize or acknowledge. She just crept into the back room. I didn't see her emerge at all, even when we left the movie theater later. Stephen's family members laughed, as we made our way to the car.

Everyone in Stephen's family towers over me. His sister is six feet tall, and his aunts are all at least five feet eight inches, so my five-foot-three-and-a-half-inch status and different skin color threw her off. It's interesting though, that she didn't ask if we were together or assume we were, because I could have been perceived as a space invader, uncomfortably too close, if we weren't together.

Love looks different. Family looks different. Sometimes its loud, sometimes quiet, sometimes your skin color doesn't match, sometimes you are adopted in, and sometimes you don't fit a perfectly curated picture that comes in a new picture frame. I learned this as we took pictures during this trip. Some of the pictures showed the tops of all of their heads cut off in order to fit my short self in, and in others, all of their heads and chest up can be seen, but I am more of a floating head in a picture. I was accepted as I was—white, short, northerner "Yankee," but still accepted. Stephen's family didn't care. They loved me and made me feel welcomed. Stephen's family never made me feel like an outcast. I once again looked up to God, grateful, and felt a deep peace for the first time in a long time.

Chapter 20

Ring in the New Year

Upon returning to Alaska, I had a bounce in my step, and my left hand had a gleam and glitter, as the light bounced off of the diamond prism. Wistfully, I gazed down at my ring. I loved everything this ring represented, and I beamed. However, not everyone shared my excitement and enthusiasm about the ring.

On our first day back at work, Sergeant Church hurried into the chapel and looked anxious.

"What did you guys do? Maybe you can put that ring in your pocket or something?"

No congratulations. No "good to have you back." Why would I want to do that? He advised me again that I should probably take off my ring.

My body stiffened. There is no rule against marrying someone in your company, or even a coworker. Church could have switched positions around for the chaplain assistants if they were worried about unfair treatment and a conflict of interest. I had worked at the other chapel before when Specialist Fox was in training. I could be switched me with him, or they could make the counseling center one area of operation and the chapel as another, as it was when I first got there. I also knew that he got his information and orders from Chaplain Eagle, who had made those changes to begin with. My future husband was already seeking advice of the brigade NCO and chaplain of the new unit about that possibility for the past month. It was almost as if people knew it wasn't right, but no one knew what could be done. The best case scenario for us was to switch job positions. Stephen felt called to help soldiers and was missing being in a line unit. Instead of helping the families of soldiers, he wanted to be work more with soldiers, and there was an available slot. We prayed about how to deal with things at work and for an answer from God for the next step to take. This seemed like the push for the step to be taken. My fiancé voluntarily agreed to go to the infantry division. Taking this position meant also taking on the knowledge of a looming separation. It was only a matter a time, serving in an infantry unit, until he deployed.

"Sergeant, this is ridiculous. Why would this important symbol, something that radiates joy, be taken away from me?"

After I refused to do as he requested, he followed up with, "It is probably a good idea to lie low and not bring attention to it. Do not tell anybody that you are engaged and who you are engaged to." He reiterated this because it looked bad for our unit and the chaplain corps. There would be too many questions. Don't tell.

Ring in the New Year

To a point, I half listened. I didn't go around proclaiming it, but I proudly wore my ring, and I sure as hell didn't hide it, or the story, once someone noticed it. Most people who worked in the chapel knew we spent a lot of time together. We were friends always, before anything. He was my best friend. Chaplain Staff and his family gushed with enthusiasm for me. His daughters told me they had a suspicion that we liked each other from the first time we met at Chaplain Sword's house. Chapel congregants asked me if there was something different about me because they said I glowed and beamed. Heck yeah, I beamed! I was marrying the man of my dreams and had my daddy's stamp of approval.

Less than three days later, I was back to work, scheduling appointments for clients and answering the phone in my office. As I hung up the phone, Chaplain Sword called me into his office. He asked me to close the door to have a heart-to-heart with me.

My heart pounded in my chest. Chaplain Sword always was warm to me, as well as the other chaplain assistants, including Stephen, but I could tell we were about to have a serious discussion. Chaplain Sword and his wife went out of the way to invite us over, to share meals together. I hung out with his children, we went to the movies, we snowboarded together, we rode four-wheelers, and we had movie and game nights. His family was so dear to me. Chaplain Sword was kind and fair, but would he side with Chaplain Eagle? My mouth became dry, and a lump formed in my throat, as I awaited the worst.

Chaplain Sword came from the same Deep South that Chaplain Eagle did. What would he say?

"I was surprised and a little hurt that you didn't tell me about your intentions with Hayes or of your engagement."

"I'm sorry. I felt it was Stephen and me against the world. I didn't know if you would understand, or stand against your supervisor or with me, a measly private?"

I paced back and forth, as I spilled the story. I shared all the garbage going on with Chaplain Eagle. Chaplain Sword leaned in nodded, eyebrows showing a bit of surprise, as I told him my plight. He threw in a few "ohs" and "uh-huhs," as a good counselor knows to do to show he was listening and engaged, without interrupting my thought process. I paused in front of his desk, and he motioned for me to sit down. I pressed back into the chair, held my breath, and rubbed my palms over my knees.

"I like both of you, and you are both great, but have you considered that if this is what it's like at the start of your relationship, there could always be something like this happening? Have you considered what your families will think? Do y'all have your parents' support? It could be very hard if not. And what if you have children? What will their lives be like? Will you be able to handle it?"

I paused as I exhaled. I felt my body concave, with the thought of future children having to deal with prejudices because of the melanin in their skin.

"Good things are worth working for, but are you willing to take that on? You will have to fight for your relationship. There will be times that it will be tough, and that's the reality. Make sure you both think things through."

He came around from behind his desk. His crystal blue eyes shone with hope and the gravity of the situation, and they broke through to my guarded heart.

"I will support you guys, but just make sure you both go into this with eyes wide open." Cue the waterworks. I had cried and prayed, many times in our office, but this time, it wasn't because it overwhelmed my heart. I jumped up, and my head felt tingly. I had an ally.

I hugged Chaplain Sword, and he patted my back. He had been my stand-in for my family, my Alaskan dad. He always asked if I wanted to be treated like a soldier or one of his daughters. I had said I wanted to be, "a soldier, sir," but there I was, feeling as if my actual dad had hugged me.

There is still, to this day, some disdain for interracial relationships in our society. Periodically, I look back on that discussion, and I know now what he was saying. Stephen and I faced prejudices and bias, sometimes ignorance, and sometimes hatred. It still pains me to see anyone who hurts in these ways. Forget it, if it's a person I love being put through that. I would much rather take on the pain than have to see it in Stephen's tired eyes. Love means baring one another's burdens, and love is always worth it.

I thought about what Chaplain Sword said. I was a little hurt and confused by the discussion at first. It shouldn't matter what a person looks like. All people are fearfully and wonderfully made. We all reflect an aspect of our Creator. Stephen did not get to decide the color of his skin when he formed in his mother's womb. I didn't either, but my skin affords me some opportunities and the benefit of the doubt, while Stephen's does not necessarily do the same. Love is what can make the difference in others' lives. Whether platonic or romantic, love means laying down your life for another. I know what freedoms I could have had if I married someone who looks like me. I would never have to second guess about being seated in the back of a restaurant, even though there were a lot of tables open in a server's area. If Stephen was white, I would not struggle with anxious thoughts for his safety when we get pulled over by the authorities. And this is coming from me as an onlooker. Usually, I am not the target of hate. I also know that I still have privileges based on how I look, and my fiancé had to deal with prejudices based on how he looked.

Still, the beauty of differences in cultures has always intrigued me. I loved Stephen for all he was, his characteristics, and his nature. When Stephen walked into the room, I felt the energy change just from his spirit. God has created an array of colors in humans, and I have always loved intertwining our arms and marveling at the contrast of our skin.

Not everyone believed that differences are beautiful, however. Less than two weeks from the time of us getting back from Christmas leave, we were once again in the line of fire.

Chapter 21

Friendly Fire

Friendly fire: getting caught in the crosshairs of a battle by someone who is supposed to be on your side.

A week after our engagement, one of my friends showed up at my barracks. She knew that Stephen and I were dating, but I had excitedly told her on the phone that we were engaged.

"Lorin, if we weren't friends, I would have knocked you out by now." She wanted me to know she disapproved and that it's best for Stephen and me to dissolve our relationship.

"Why? Do you have feelings for Stephen?"

"No, but there are not too many good ones left."

"What?"

Would I need to worry about my friend fighting me because the person I loved had more melanin in his skin? I did not work through it with this friend as I may have now. I just stopped talking to her because I was deeply hurt. I thought that because she was friends with me, this wouldn't be an issue. She was okay with me dating people who were brown skinned, but she was not okay with us getting married. That would take him off the market, and she told me that, as a black woman, she had fewer options than me, so I could just find another guy. This was so strange to me. I had only seen this in movies before. In New York, I had somehow thought things were more progressive, and here it was in real life. In different friendships, it seemed race was not only a small consideration, but a vital one.

After Stephen's transition into the new unit, he befriended a co-worker, Teddy. Stephen invited him and his wife to dinner at our house. I had never met him or his wife. Teddy came into our house and, upon entering it and seeing me, declared he didn't like white people. My eyes popped out of my head, and my mouth dropped open, as I wondered why he was there. He didn't have white friends. His experience with white people was one of racism, hate, and not being welcomed. Stephen hadn't mentioned that I was white, and it was a shocker.

It took years for me to like Teddy.

At first, I felt as if every bad experience Teddy had ever experienced from a white person was taken out on me. I was defensive, but eventually, I learned to see his perspective and even accepted whatever unintended harm I might have contributed at any point in my life. While I didn't always agree with his opinions, I did appreciate his honesty. We had many historical discussions about the implications of race. I learned about his childhood, which made me get a glimpse into how his beliefs were formed. I learned that he had encounters with the KKK. I learned that for him, Stephen and my relationship was his first experience of a relationship like ours, one that wasn't formed because we had a "shotgun wedding." He was intrigued that we just found each other and loved each other, that there wasn't a caveat. His wife and I became good friends, and with time, I realized he was actually a great friend to Stephen, and he had some qualities that Stephen saw in him. Since Stephen was a good judge of character, I thought I should try to be less guarded and ask more questions, just learn from Teddy. Eventually, I think he grew to like and accept me as a friend, and I grew to call him friend as well.

Sam was one of the soldiers we worked with. Stephen was his first black friend. Stephen, Sam, and Teddy had a ton in common, as they loved cars and joking around, they were soldiers, and they liked the same movies. These two friends of Stephen's started out with a bit of bad blood between them because they knew where the other came from. One was from Alabama, on the east side, and one was from northern Florida. Teddy and Sam knew the area where the other lived and the racial tension that existed in their respective towns. They were leery of each other. Sam had heard stories of Teddy hating all white people. Others had portrayed Sam as racist to Teddy. These two never met each other before, but I could feel that tension brewing when we had them both over at the same time to hang out.

These friendships were some of the most interesting opportunities to bridge the gap. As an interracial couple, we decided we would not have two separate friend groups, needing to double every event. We invited Teddy and Sam to be in the same spaces, and over time, they were okay with each other. While it was uncomfortable and made for some awkwardness, it was beautiful to witness walls coming down. To this day, Sam and Teddy don't agree on many things—politics, religion, even racial problems in this country—but it seems they have a mutual respect now. Today these guys are still two of Stephen's best friends.

We base a lot on our experiences and quick judgments, sometimes from appearance alone. We are assumed to be more comfortable with people who look the same as us. I started this joke with Stephen that maybe we should introduce ourselves ridiculously, such as, "Have you met my black fiancé?" or, "Did you know Lorin is white?" It's not that we didn't know we were different. We weren't color blind, and contrary to popular statements, people do see color. If you have your physical sight, you see color. The thing is, we should be color acceptant. Stephen had all the characteristics of what I wanted a husband to be, as well as what I didn't even understand I wanted but needed. Stephen was the man I loved, and he happened to black. Likewise, I am the woman he loved, and I happen to be white.

When people said to me they didn't know my fiancé was black, or they had no idea when they met me that my partner was black, I didn't know what to say at first. It baffled me because I questioned what one should look like if a significant other is from a different culture than one's own. Should I have to try to assimilate and become someone different? I started to push back after this became a recurring theme after meeting people. Moving forward, I always questioned people with, "What should I have looked like or acted like, so you would know?"

Well, what should I or anyone look like or be like, if my significant other looks different than me? The hope is that people will confront what biases they may have and question why they feel they can know everything about a person in a relationship based on appearance. If I am different from my significant other, should I have to blend in and become someone different?

No. Just because the person I love looks different, it doesn't mean I change who I am completely at the core, my identity. Of course,

Friendly Fire

having someone close to me who lived a different life challenges me and has me reexamining the lens through which I view life. I now have someone who can help me check my ignorance and naiveté. It's not a one-time thing. It's a continual learning process.

One time, I asked Stephen to drive home from our friend's house. I wanted him to drive, because I was tired, so I climbed into the passenger seat.

"I can't. If I get pulled over, I don't have my wallet."

I turned to look at him. "It's no big deal. That's happened to me before. You can just tell them you forgot it, and it should be fine. As long as you're not driving ridiculous, they won't even pull you over."

Stephen laughed at me and paused, searching my eyes. I stared back, confused.

"Sure… for you, but not for me."

As he pointed to his arm, I realized, in that moment, it can be easy for me to forget. I don't live his daily experience. He had told me stories, before I ever saw instances of him being profiled and pulled over for no reason. His experience of being harassed because he worked at a dealership and they had thought there was no way a black man could drive such a nice car, so they pulled him over. I thought about all the things I take for granted and had to apologize for being insensitive. I switched seats with him.

When summer rolled around, Stephen's friend, Dameon, was having a barbecue. Dameon was a fellow soldier, and he invited Stephen and some other coworkers, along with their spouses. When we showed up, it was just the men grilling and hanging out. The significant others were on their way back from a store run, but they hadn't gotten back yet. Ty, James, and Isaiah talked and joked and laughed while they grilled and told stories. Ty said they needed more charcoal, so Dameon and Stephen took a trip to the gas station to get some more. Five minutes after Stephen and Dameon left, the wives arrived.

As soon as the car's engine turned off, and the car doors closed, the mood shifted. Ty wouldn't look at me. Now all three guys' countenance changed, and they made themselves busy with grilling and stopped talking to me. That's weird. I went from the kitchen to the dining table. I had met none of the ladies before, so I introduced myself to the first lady I saw, asking if she needed help with the grocery bags in her hand. Her bronzed skin shone in the streams of light pouring into the window. She seemed a bit startled, but she was cordial. I sat back down because I didn't want to crowd them at the door.

Then, two more ladies trickled into the house. I jumped up and introduced myself, and one woman played with her braids, glanced back at her friend, then at me, and didn't say anything. I introduced myself again, apologizing if I had interrupted them. Maybe they were still talking. The woman whose house I was in completely ignored my existence. She talked through me, and, from that point on, looked through me, as if I wasn't there. She didn't make comments, positive or negative, to me or about me, but she just completely ignored me. At one point, she turned her chair 180 degrees away from the table to the other two ladies who were talking in the living room, shifting her back toward me!

I was shocked. I was indignant at this treatment. If I could have, I would have run out the door, jumped in the car, and left, but I had to wait for Stephen to come back. It was an agonizing twenty minutes later when he showed up. By that time, the lady of the house had taken the other ladies upstairs, and I was sitting at the table alone. Stephen came in the door with a hamburger, and I told him I needed to leave as soon as possible.

Friendly Fire

"I'm not welcome here. I can't stay."

When we got in the car, I told him the details of the odd encounter and then it hit me. I gasped, "Is this what it's normally like for you? Do you feel silenced, ignored, or cast out?"

"Sometimes."

I was the only white person at this barbecue, and because everyone was too uncomfortable or didn't want to ruffle feathers, no one said anything else to me. I was invisible. It left such an impact on me. My heart was heavy. I saw a glimpse of what life was like when you don't fit into the majority, and people don't pull up a chair for you to sit at their table, let alone give you space at the table. Sometimes, that is why people have to bring their own tables. How beautiful would it be if those of us already sitting at a table could pull up a chair and not only make space, but welcome someone different from us to fill that space?

Chapter 22

Welcome to the Infantry

After we had been home from our engagement about two weeks, Stephen and I were back into our routine. In the mornings, after our post-PT shower, Stephen and I went to breakfast at the DFAC (cafeteria). I called Stephen to let him know I was starting my car to warm it up. The person who parked next to me parked close, so as I tried to climb back out, I slammed my head on the corner of the door. I felt lightheaded; I had knocked myself pretty good, so I decided to just kneel and put my head back on the seat for a minute. I closed my eyes for a minute and then opened them. I stood up and realized about half the cars that had parked outside were now gone. That's weird. I made my way to the stairs, and my head was throbbing. As I approached the door, the hallway seemed to be moving in waves. I used the wall to make my way down the hall to his room on the opposite side. I knocked on the door and steadied myself.

Welcome to the Infantry

Stephen opened the door.

"Hey, what the heck happened to you?"

"What do you mean?"

"You have blood dripping down your face!"

I stepped inside his room and went over to his bathroom mirror. The blood was running down the middle of my brows, all the way down my nose.

"Oh, I hit my head on my car door."

"What? You're kidding me! You okay? You have to be more careful."

He drove to the dining facility because I still didn't feel well. When we got to breakfast, I rehashed the story again. He laughed in disbelief.

"Lorin, I don't think you just put your head down for a minute. If that happened right after you called me, it was thirty minutes before you knocked on my door."

"That can't be. It was just a minute."

"No. It was a half an hour. I think you better go get checked out at the hospital."

I didn't want to go to the hospital, but he insisted I get checked out because I might have a concussion. After signing in at the hospital, I had to retell the story several times. I tried to explain my story in a low voice, so no one could overhear, but it didn't matter. The medics thought it was hoot, and every time a new person came in the room, they said, "Go ahead… tell the story of how you knocked yourself out."

I went home with a concussion and Stephen took care of me.

He had to wake me up every hour to make sure I was okay.

A few days passed, and we were back at parade rest in front of Sergeant Church. "So, now that you guys are engaged, you cannot be working together. We will have to figure it out."

My body stiffened, and I could feel my ears get hot. There is no rule against marrying someone in your company or even a coworker. Most times, they switched it, so spouses weren't working with each other, so it didn't affect the unit. Chaplain Eagle could have switched him with the chaplain assistant at the other chapel. He could have just changed the roles in his position, so he was not responsible for me, so there was no conflict of interest.

My fiancé was already seeking wise counsel from leaders of the new unit about the possibility to move there, and he'd been looking into it for the previous month. Stephen felt called to help soldiers and was missing being in a line unit. Instead of helping the families of soldiers, he wanted to work more with soldiers, and there was an available slot. He had been waiting for the infantry brigade to get back from spending time with their families, as they had just gotten home from deployment. We prayed about how to deal with things at work, as well as an answer from God about next step to take. This seemed like the push for the step to be taken. My fiancé agreed to go to the infantry division, knowing it meant he would deploy.

We had to plan what our next steps were. We could live on post once we were married, but we would then have to put our name on the housing list, which goes by priority, and that could take some time. We had time. We had at least a few months to look for an apartment while

Welcome to the Infantry

we lived in the barracks, right?

Sergeant Church came knocking on the door a week later, while Stephen and I were eating lunch in his room.

"Hey, Hayes. I need to talk to you. Since you two are getting married, you will have to leave the barracks. You can no longer live here."

"Sergeant?"

"Chaplain Eagle says you have until this weekend to leave."

There was one major problem, though. Stephen was not a part of the new unit yet. He was waiting on his orders. He had to have orders to sign into the unit, so was unable to live in the new unit's barracks until then. Sergeant Church's eyes shifted left and right and then looked down. A flash of uncertainty swept across his face, his tone deflated. His body sunk inward at first, but then he cleared his throat and pressed his shoulders back, as Stephen faced him.

"Where will I go, Sergeant?"

"I don't know. Maybe check with the unit you will go to."

Stephen's unit didn't have a place for him. They weren't in a rush because he was already in our unit with a barracks room.

I glared at the doorway and bit my lip. No one had a problem when a married soldier and his wife stayed in the barracks before, all the while collecting a housing allowance for being married. Our unit and Chaplain Eagle let them stay for six months, waiting for housing. That was illegal because that's double dipping—getting to live in the barracks with free room and board and pocketing money given for the housing allowance. There is also the rule that the barracks was only for single soldiers or geographic bachelors (those with spouses and kids in another state) to live in the government quarters and barracks, not civilians. There is no rule that two engaged soldiers cannot occupy the same barracks. I didn't understand.

"Wait, Sergeant. When should I expect to be kicked out?"

"Well, Hayes is going to another unit, but you are still in our unit, so you will stay here. But as soon as you guys are married, you won't be able to live here either."

Without our marriage license, the Army would not allow us to live in military housing. Since we were getting married anyway, we decided we could look into getting an apartment before our wedding date. The commanding officer had to sign off on paperwork to receive money for the housing allowance because when soldiers were in the barracks, it counted as room and board, and we needed an exception to the policy. Guess who was the officer that had to sign the letter... none other than Chaplain Eagle. We decided to see if anyone would rent to us without the letter.

I jiggled my leg, as we drove to the first apartment. We brought our pay statements, so the apartment manager could see we could afford to rent a small apartment.

"Tell me it's going to be okay. We can make it work, right?"

Stephen grabbed my hand and squeezed it. "We will make it work. Don't worry."

I smiled and squeezed his hand, as he helped me out of the car. We were going to be okay. We interlocked hands, as we walked into the housing office for the first apartment.

"We would like to rent an apartment."

"Sorry. Without being married, without the form for exception to policy from your commander, without the housing allowance, we won't rent to you. You need to make three times the amount of the rent."

"But we have money saved up, and we can give you a deposit."

"Sorry. We can't help you. You need to make more money. Come back when you're married."

We went to other apartments that were available, where we had three times the amount of money for them, and we had enough to do a double deposit, but all the available apartment complexes said they wouldn't rent us an apartment together, because we were not married yet.

The apartment complexes didn't have to because under the law, they only had to lease to common law couples or couples with a marriage license. Some wouldn't rent to Stephen alone because they said he didn't qualify on a single soldier's paycheck, even though he said he could put down a double deposit. There was no good reasonable explanation. No one would rent to us or him.

Everywhere we went to, we had a similar conversation.

"Well, what about just renting to him and then I can live in the barracks until we are married and add me to lease later. That way, he has a place to stay."

"Now that we know that you guys are trying to live together, how do we know you won't just get it in his name and still live there?"

"Well, because I said I wouldn't. I still can live on base, but he can't. Can you please just rent him an apartment?"

CAMOUFLAGED LOVE

"Sorry. We cannot help you. Our hands are tied."

We thought it might be a week or two, but it took longer for the new unit to be reflagged and renamed under the new brigade. For almost three months, Stephen waited on orders. He had nowhere to go. Our friends, Sam and Lee, opened their home to Stephen. They gave him the only space they had, their basement, and an air mattress near the washer and dryer. All of Stephen's belongings were stacked in the corner on one side. Sam and Lee could have been kicked out of housing and fined for allowing someone to stay there, as it was unauthorized. I thank God that they took that risk and that they did not suffer any repercussions. And I thank God for the friendships that are real and not just in it for the good times, but also for our lowest moments.

Chapter 23

Female Soldier

"71% of female veterans develop PTSD due to sexual assault within the ranks."
-The Pink Berets

As time went on, our company dwindled from a few platoons to one. The Army was phasing out a lot of different MOSs (military occupation specialty jobs). So, my air traffic control friends, even supply soldiers, administration soldiers, and the soldier firefighters, were told to PCS (permanent change their duty station), reclass into a different job, or to get out of the Army. Some of them got out of the Army and stayed at Fort Wainwright doing their same job, just as a civilian. It came down to where there were just chaplains and chaplain assistants in my unit, our sergeant major, and a speckling of administrative soldiers. When my friends, Jenica and Kay, left, one for the next station, and one leaving the Army and going back the civilian jobs, the administrative jobs became civilian jobs, and I was the only female in my unit of nine people.

Being a female in the Army sometimes felt like a novelty. From my perspective, there were two groups the males used to categorize female soldiers. There were the ones who were just accepted as one of the guys. I realize this is a stereotype, but these girls watched NASCAR and drank beers with the mechanics, and were more of what people considered a tomboy. Then there were the females who dressed more feminine, maybe did their makeup, maybe not, but were more girly. I always felt as if I was somewhere in the middle of these contrived groups. I didn't watch NASCAR, but I could easily hang out with the guys. For four years in the Army, you wouldn't catch me without makeup in my uniform, and when I was out of uniform, I always had my hair down out of that uptight bun. Most of the soldiers were male on post, so I tended to have more male friends, and my female friends were other soldiers or family members of the soldiers I was also friends with. I never wanted or expected special treatment because I was a female. I just wanted equal treatment. I did my best to have my short stubby legs keep up on our company runs. I maxed out my pushups and always passed my PT tests. I never felt as if I was a part of one or the other group. I don't feel that people can or should classify women in any arena. We are all different, and I hate that my fellow sisters-in-arms had to be classified as anything but soldiers.

Regardless of how a woman looks or acts, it seems to be the universal experience that outrageous things happen to women in our world. The Army is no exception. One time, I went on a mandatory trip to Seward. I didn't want to go. I don't like ice fishing, and I don't like the outdoorsy things that were going to be a part of the trip, but the company made me go. I brought my CDs and CD player because I just planned to chill and listen to my music. One of the guys asked me if I could lend him a CD and asked me to bring it to his room. I walked down the hall and knocked on his door. He asked me to come in and then flashed me, with his pants around his ankles. I guess this was supposed to seduce me. I bolted.

Another time, I helped my good friend, Specialist King, get ready for his deployment. Like me, he was a master of procrastination, and he had to get his stuff packed and cleaned out of his barracks, into storage, and he had to pack his gear. I drove my car to his barracks where another friend, Alesha, and I were planning to help him get ready. As soon as I stepped out of the car, I heard the gaggle of soldiers laughing and joking outside the barracks. There were about twenty infantrymen. I thought nothing of it at first. Everyone got to hang out before they were deployed, until the catcalling began. It made me so uncomfortable, but I ignored them, while my face flushed. Then, some of them started waltzing toward me.

"Hey. It's our last night before we leave, and we want it to be enjoyable. Why don't you come over here and help us out."

"Yeah, we need one last good f@#$."

"Don't be scared. We just want one last good time."

Maintaining eye contact with me, some soldiers swarmed closer to me. I flew back into my car and locked it. My hands shook, as I dropped my phone twice and scrambled, searching for my friend's number.

"Can you please come out here to get me? There are a bunch of guys out here, and they are making me feel scared."

My friend strolled out of the barracks, with a few other friends in tow, to walk me inside through a different door on the side. Still, catcalling and vulgar comments spewed from their lips about how much I would like what they would do to me.

Or, there was the time when a soldier befriended me. One day, he gave me a ride. He was supposed to drop me back off at an Army function, but he suddenly realized he needed to stop for something at his home. He said he needed something, but he had to find it, and it may take a few minutes. He asked if I wanted water, and he invited me in. I went in. He showed me around his house. I admired his pictures of his kids. They were adorable. I had met his wife and kids at an Army function a few months prior.

"If you think that's cute, you should see the pictures at the top of stairs." I smiled to myself, as I ascended the stairs. I have always loved kids, and these kids were adorable. When I got to the picture, I glanced at my cell phone and saw there was no signal there. It was then that I realized he was behind me. I felt a lump in my throat, as I now realized I had not heard anyone in the house.

"Where's your wife today?" I asked as nonchalantly as I could muster.

"Oh she is not here." My chest tightened.

"Oh, so where are your kids then?"

"They are at a relative's house."

"Okay. I'm ready to go." I started to walk toward the stairs to head back down. He caught my arm.

"No. I want to finish showing the rest of my house, since we're here, and then we can go." He put his other hand around the small of my back and pushed me along. My mind raced. What is going on? Why are we here? He guided me into the center of the next room.

"And this is my bedroom." The door shut, and then the sound of the lock clicking echoed in my ear.

I whipped around. "What are you doing?"

He came toward me.

"Come on… you know why you're here. But you're a good girl, so I know you have to pretend this isn't what you want."

I stepped back "No. I don't know what you are doing, but whatever you are thinking, the answer is no. Please take me back to the barracks."

It wasn't what I wanted.

He was stronger than me. I said no. I said no again and again. I tried to reason with him.

"NO! Wait! What about your wife and kids? What will she think? Please don't do this."

I began to sob. It didn't matter. He said it was too late to have a conscience. He convinced himself that I wanted this to happen. I had gone in the car with him, after all. I wanted this because I went with him.

His actions left a scar on my heart long after his fingerprints and body etched an invisible wound on my soul. I was confused and scared. I didn't tell anyone. I didn't think anyone would believe me. Worse, I didn't think anyone cared about me. He was a respected leader. I believed I would be the one in trouble. The military is the only institution I know of where infidelity is a punishable offense. Would they believe that there was no consent? He was in a position of authority, and I was a lower-enlisted person. I felt helpless.

Even married soldiers didn't want their wives to go to their offices. There were all males in the infantry unit. When my future husband finally switched to the infantry unit, I had to call, so he knew I was coming, so he could either meet me outside to walk me to his office, which was only the second door down the hallway but fifty feet from the reception desk, or so he could be on the lookout for me. Soldiers sized me up and down, undressing me with their eyes. I tried a few different outfits to see if I could make it stop. I went in my uniform; it didn't matter. I went in the rattiest workout clothes; it didn't matter. I went with jeans and a T-shirt; it didn't matter. I didn't dare go in a dress or skirt. The men stuck their heads out of their offices and gawked. Some had the audacity to whistle or say inappropriate things. Besides it being far too common, it's also hard to report things to higher officials when sometimes, they perpetuate the behavior, or at least tolerate what's happening. If you spoke up, you were not tough enough. It was guys just being guys. I never spoke up. I had seen other females try. The unspoken ramification was to be labeled as difficult to work with, or carry the stigma of someone everyone needs to cater to. When females spoke up, they were dismissed. What did she do to warrant that attention?

This is not meant to paint my fellow veterans with one swoop of a brush. I have plenty of brother veterans who have stuck up for what's right, who have stood for the values that the Army esteems. The Army and military expect soldiers to behave in higher moral standing, one of respect, integrity, duty and discipline. I made some of my best and longest life friends from my military service, the majority being men.

Female Soldier

The bigger problem is accountability and having leaders with integrity who won't look the other way, who are willing to risk their own likeability and sometimes even advancement in their careers because it was not a simple thing. I can see how that was hard for someone to make that choice, and I vowed to always be the person I wished was there for me.

Whether you are single or married, these types of assault, harassment, and attacks are too common. I have never met a female soldier who did not have at least one experience of harassment, whether "minor" or more serious. I learned from myself and other women, we often quiet that inkling that something might be wrong. I believe God gave us instincts to help us. Not every instance did I have a bad feeling, but I think as women, we are taught not to trust ourselves too much. We are labeled as too emotional, too sensitive, or too much, especially in male-dominated spaces. Even though I may still look for the good in everyone, the most important thing I learned as a woman was to trust my instincts, and that I needed to carefully use discernment.

Chapter 24

JAG

Judge Advocate Generals (JAG) are officers in the U.S. Military that serve as legal advisors and to the command. Complaints of misconduct or behavior are sent to the JAG office, where the lawyers and paralegals investigate and prosecute as necessary.

From the time Stephen and I got back from leave, engaged, until the date of our wedding, word from my informant, my paralegal friend, King, was that Chaplain Eagle was in an uproar. He tried every angle to get us in trouble; he wanted to give us Article 15s. Article 15 are non-judicial punishments, to include loss of rank and pay, potentially discharged and termination from service. If we were to receive article 15s they could result in the worst case scenario, a dishonorable discharge which makes it nearly impossible to get a job.

He was up in the JAG office every two days with a fresh idea of how to get us kicked out of the Army. Most companies have policies on fraternization, so that bosses don't take advantage of their subordinates, or that there is not unfair treatment because someone is dating the boss. The Army is no different. Army disciplinary procedures are based on the grade (rank) of the officer who is filing. The higher in rank, the more the propensity to get in trouble. The higher the rank, the higher the stakes were. Stephen and I were both lower enlisted. At the beginning of our relationship, he was a specialist, and I was a private first class, which was one rank below. After getting engaged, we were both specialists, and, therefore, the same rank. Either way we were legally allowed to date. The technicality and trickiness of the situation was he put Stephen in charge of two areas and said I had to answer to him, so he was "acting" as an NCO (noncommissioned officer) and supervisor of me.

"AR 600-200 paragraph 4-14, says fraternization between different ranks is illegal, and he is her supervisor as he is in a role of supervisor."

"That doesn't count, since they are both junior enlisted soldiers," JAG said.

"Well, what about the fact that I told them not to date because they work together? They disobeyed a direct order from a field grade officer. Article 91 states that if soldiers willfully disobey orders, display indifferent, insolence and impertinence, contempt or disrespect to the rank and state of the officer."

"There is nothing in the regulation saying people in the same unit can't date if they are peers."

"Well, the fact is that their relationship was a secret. That can get them in trouble."

"No," JAG said, "because when you asked them, they didn't lie to an officer, which would be a punishable offense. They came out with the truth."

Chaplain Eagle frequented their office, talking to all the different JAG officers and paralegals, trying to get a new idea on how to prosecute.

He was angrier than he was smart, cunning, and determined. Chaplain Eagle knew how to cover himself. He made things extremely hard for Stephen and me at work.

In the midst of the stress of UCMJ hanging above our heads, my dear Chaplain Sword came up on orders, and I mourned his leaving. I would miss him. I loved his family. They became a second family to me. He would no longer be there to run interference. The workload was piling on, and I could no longer take college classes either. I stayed late, came in early, and was unable to leave for my lunch break most days, as I was covering two or three areas as everyone attended their schools.

After all the craziness of Stephen getting kicked out of the barracks, I felt miserable. I kept thinking, with Stephen leaving the unit, I had no one to confide in during the day to see if what I was being told to do was on the "up and up." I wanted to go to school to become an NCO. I wanted to go to specialized chaplain assistant training, so I could change jobs, maybe take the funds management course to become a finance manager for the chaplain funds (bonus being not working in the same area of operation anymore). I wanted to get training in all kinds of things. To be competitive in my job or go for a promotion and to have access to more opportunities, school is necessary. The big boss denied me every single school I wanted to go to because I was "too invaluable." I bitterly watched the other chaplain assistants in my unit go to schools, some of them gone for months in back-to-back training.

One day, while I was cleaning the chapel floor, hanging my head, another chaplain assistant, Sergeant Wash, wandered inside to the chapel to reserve it for a function.

"Good morning, Sergeant."

"Good morning."

I looked down at my feet. I tried to hold it together, as it hadn't really been a good morning.

"Warrior, your eyes look sad, and you aren't smiling like usual. What's wrong?" Her voice was sincere. Maybe I could tell her? No, it's probably better not get into the details, and I don't really know her.

"Sergeant, I am just having a hard time and some problems, but I'll get through it," I assured her.

"Can you tell me more? Maybe I can help."

I hesitated, but her brown eyes searched my face with a look of concern and kindness I hadn't felt in awhile. She offered to listen to me, and after all, this is what being a chaplain assistant was about. Since she was both a female and a minority, I thought maybe, just maybe, she could help me. Surely, she had navigated some of the mistreatment as a woman and as a black woman.

I told her of all the things that had happened with mistreatment from leadership that seemed to come down from Chaplain Eagle. I explained how they tried to stop us from dating and how Chaplain Eagle was busy trying to get us in a world of trouble. I explained how my leaders and coworkers said I was being too sensitive, and when I came to them with some injustice and I talked about it, he asked me if I was just "PMS-ing." I explained how mortifying it was being questioned, trying to explain, and having men debate about my period problems.

"Sergeant, they thought I was faking it, so they insisted on knowing why I needed to go to the sick hall so frequently. I take all these different meds that should help women during their cycle, but nothing over the counter helps." (Years later I found out I had cysts from an endocrine disorder. That's why I didn't get my period for months and would later bleed to the point of my body being rundown for several weeks at a time, which contributed to the infertility, insulin, and metabolism issues, but I didn't know that then).

"I have these debilitating cramps and intense bleeding that sometimes leaves me curled up in a ball." She nodded in understanding. "After going back to these military doctors repeatedly, doing blood work that doesn't show anything, and receiving test results that are inconclusive, I return to work. Then, everyone assumes I am exaggerating my issues. When I had no choice but to again go to sick call because of the pain and feeling terrible, I am told by the doctor that they are just cramps, and I'll be fine, and he prescribes me strong meds."

"Wow."

"So then I come back to work, but I cannot take the medicine because then I cannot work. The doctor keeps giving my Tylenol with codeine, and you cannot operate heavy machinery or drive on that stuff. Besides, other soldiers in our unit make racist and sexist comments, even when I've asked them to stop because it bothered me. I am told I can't take a joke. I am told it's just a period. Other women don't get to call out of work every month, and you won't be able to either."

Her nostrils flared. She looked as if she was trying hard to maintain her military composure as a senior leader in the Army, but she was no doubt angry.

I was just tired of it, and I had nowhere to turn to. Our commander of our unit was in Fort Richardson in Anchorage because the Army changed most of the jobs in our unit to civilian positions, instead of active duty soldiers. The Army decided one commander could oversee a unit from eight hours away. Our local chain of command consisted of the garrison sergeant major over the post, garrison commander over the post, and the chaplains and chaplain assistants in the unit. Everyone else had been discharged from the Army or changed duty stations.

"What should I do, Sergeant?"

She placed her arm on my shoulder and looked me square in my face.

"Don't worry. I'll help you. I'm going to go visit them and have a talk with them. This should not happen." Her voice commanded authority. It reminded me of when my mom caught me talking in church and gave me a look that I better get it together because she wasn't to be tested.

    I felt better as she walked out of the chapel. Even though she was from a different unit, I thought that with her being a sergeant and her being a female chaplain assistant, she could tell me what to do, maybe talk to my supervisor. What I hadn't known was that she was already having problems with Chaplain Eagle.

Chapter 25

Whistleblower

A few days later, Sergeant Church marched into the chapel with Sergeant Drum, as I swept the floor. Sergeant Church's eyes furrowed. "I need to talk to you right now." He motioned toward my office. My heart pounded and felt as if it was moving up into my throat. My legs felt wobbly, as my mind raced. What was coming?

He closed the door and ripped into me.

"What did you do? You screwed up. You talked to Sergeant Wash. That female sergeant is not to be trusted! We are a family, and our stuff needs to stay inside our family, without our dirty laundry being aired. Chaplain Eagle is pissed at you, and Sergeant Wash, well, she is no good. She is always trying to get Chaplain Eagle into trouble. She has been recording him and their conversations. He doesn't like to be made to look bad. We are a family here. This is not how families work."

He went on, but I couldn't digest it all. So, Sergeant Wash had confronted Chaplain Eagle with what we talked about and how I was being mistreated, but she said she would help. This wasn't helpful. I had no warning. I felt betrayed. I lost all my military bearing, and I raised my voice.

"Sergeant, I explained I had tried to talk to you. She is a fellow chaplain assistant and wanted to help because I didn't feel that they were treating me right, or Stephen. I have tried to talk to you many times!" I threw my hands up in the air. "Why can't you guys be happy for us? Why doesn't Chaplain Eagle like Stephen? Why doesn't he want us to be together? Why does he have a problem with our interracial relationship?"

"It has nothing to do with color. Chaplain Eagle isn't racist. He has a few black friends."

"Well, he sure doesn't seem to act like he is okay with us dating!"

"Sorry you feel that way. That's not what's happening here. You're too sensitive. If you have a problem, you need to take it up with me or Chaplain Eagle."

"Really, Sergeant?!? I have plenty of times! I speak up when anyone in our unit says something out of line, and I am told that it's because I'm a woman, I'm too sensitive, and I have to get over it."

The other sergeant's eyes bulged, and he raised eyebrows, but he kept silent.

I cried, but this time, it was not because I was sad but because I was furious. I didn't want him to think that because I was crying, I was weak. I snapped my head back to glare at his face.

"Sergeant, I have been telling you when you or our coworkers were disrespectful to women, or making racist comments that are out of line, or when you've ask me if I am on my cycle. You cannot ask me if

I'm on my period! You cannot ask me inappropriate questions and say statements, like asking if I have a thing for black guys, and even though Stephen is not in our unit, he is still getting mistreated still by Chaplain Eagle!"

Hot, angry tears stained my cheeks

"This isn't fair how you guys are treating us, and what else am I supposed to do? I only wanted help."

Now I was a traitor. I was supposed to keep it in the family and not air out our dirty laundry. Sergeant Church wrinkled his forehead and pointed to the counseling form he slapped on the desk.

"Under no circumstances are you to talk to Sergeant Wash or anyone else besides me and Chaplain Eagle about chaplain and chaplain's assistant matters. We keep it in the family. Do you hear me? That's a direct order!"

He motioned for me to sign the counseling statement. I checked the box that I disagreed with his statement and watched as his nostrils flared.

He warned one last time before briskly turning on his heels and shut the glass door of the chapel.

I resisted the urge to knock everything off my desk with one big swoop; instead, I closed my office door and screamed into my arms on my desk. Then I took a few deep breaths, and after I could gather of my wits, I jotted down the conversation that just happened. Then I called Stephen.

My stomach did a flip when Stephen said, "Love, you need to file a complaint. I think it's time you take it to Sergeant Major."

Sergeant Major Swamp attended the very services Chaplain Eagle preached at. Would he believe me? Would he care? Would I be in more trouble? I tightened my grip on my desk phone. There is an open-door policy in the Army that allows you direct access to talk to the commander, first sergeant, sergeant major, etc., or higher ups. But the rule in the Army is that you go through your chain of command first. Otherwise, you will get chewed up and spit out. But what do you do when your chain of command is part of the problem? What do you do if they aren't protecting you?

I almost threw up as our call connected. My mouth was dry, as I tried not to let my voice crack. I started pacing back and forth in my office. I hoped it would go straight to voicemail, but no such luck. He picked up on the third ring.

"Sergeant Major Swamp."

"Uh, Sergeant Major, um… I've been having some problems. I really need to talk to you. I tried to solve it at the lowest level and use the chain of command, but there was no one left to help."

"This sounds serious. What is it regarding?"

Whistleblower

I took a deep inhale of air. "My chaplain and my chain of command, Sergeant Major. Um… unfair treatment. And I know there is the open-door policy, and no one else can help me."

I felt my stomach flip flop, as I remembered how every Sunday I saw Sergeant Major attending services, those same services that Chaplain Eagle preached, how they seemed to be pals.

"Do you want me to come to your office to talk, or do you want to come to my office, Soldier?"

His voice reminded me of my dad. He sounded like he cared.

I paused, choking back tears.

"Sergeant Major, would it be okay to meet me somewhere besides our offices? I don't want anyone to know we are meeting."

I bit my lip. I could not meet with him at the chapel because it wouldn't be confidential; there were others who worked there and people frequently popping in unannounced. Sergeant Major's office was in the same building as Chaplain Eagle. I knew anyone in his office could see me or my car in the parking lot from their corner office.

"Sure. We can meet at the Enlisted Club on post at 1200 hours."

I sighed heavily. "Thank you, Sergeant Major."

"Roger. See you then."

I felt hopeful. He was willing to listen. Maybe he could help! I quickly texted Stephen and my sister to pray for me, as I collapsed into my office chair. I threw a Hail Mary up to the sky, with the only words I could muster "Jesus, help."

Sergeant Major Swamp met me at the Enlisted Club, in an empty room, filled with stacked tables and chairs, with three tables set out with a few chairs around each. Luckily, I had written down the details of situation, so I couldn't mess this up. With trembling hands and between tears, I rattled off my story from the very beginning. I didn't leave out anything. I ended my story with my engagement to Stephen.

"Sergeant major, I want to get out of here. It's hostile." My hands trembled, as he sat forward in his chair.

"Specialist Hayes, it's up to you. I will support you, but it's ultimately your choice. Do you want to think about it? You can file an IG complaint."

"No. I don't want them to make it worse."

"They can't legally do anything that's backlash for you speaking up. Retaliation is against the Army regulations. I'll support your decision."

"Sergeant major, I just want the madness to stop. I don't want to get anyone in trouble, as long as they stop."

I toyed with the idea of having Sergeant Church inspected, but he wasn't the man behind the curtain, the one calling the shots.

"Sergeant major, can you just talk to Chaplain Church, so he stops?"

As for Chaplain Eagle, I wanted to file an IG report on him. I didn't want him to do this to others. An Inspector General investigates grievances in which fraud, abuse, or threats to morale or safety are concerned. Complaints are protected communications under the Whilstleblower Protection Act. But this was no ordinary soldier. This was a chaplain. The dilemma was the concern about who would want to work with me. Would they indeed think that I am too soft? He could destroy my military career. What about the name of the chaplaincy? Would soldiers feel safe to come to the other chaplains for help? Would anyone trust me?

The problem was there wasn't any evidence that I could provide against Chaplain Eagle. His prior training as Special Forces served him well. There were no direct emails, so there wasn't a paper trail. He sent the sergeants in my unit to deliver the blows. He was a colonel. He was the chaplain. What would happen to me? My shoulders collapsed. What could I do at this point? It was his word against mine.

"Sergeant major, I don't have any evidence against him directly. I guess the only thing I can think of is you talking to them because I just want it to stop. I don't know what difference an IG complaint will make."

He nodded in agreement.

Sergeant Major fulfilled his promise and spoke to both Chaplain Eagle and Sergeant Church within a matter of days. Sergeant Church apologized, and by word of mouth, I heard Sergeant Wash deployed. I never heard from her again.

Chapter 26

Paperwork

A few weeks into January, and during the Chaplain Eagle's Monday meeting, we received some news. We were getting a new incoming sergeant who was going to fill Stephen's spot after he moved over to the infantry division, and she would be in charge of me. I crossed my fingers and prayed to God that this was an answer to my prayers.

By the time I got back to Alaska after our engagement, we had picked our wedding date, June 30, a day after Stephen's birthday. I joked that I was the best present Stephen was ever going to get, and that way, we could remember the date. In the months leading up to our wedding, I called to ask our family friend, Pastor Bill, to officiate. He said he would, but he required couples to do premarital counseling. We worked directly with the chaplains, so we thought it was a conflict of interest to go through one of them for counseling. Instead, we found a local church off post that our coworker Specialist Spark attended, and he vouched for us, so we could attend sessions that are typically only for members.

For twelve weeks, we attended premarital counseling in person and followed up weekly with phone conferences with Pastor Bill. Premarital counseling was eye opening for me. We talked about things we wouldn't have thought of and learned a bit about unspoken rules that we follow from our own families. In my Stephen's family, he grew up with some expectations for mealtime, that they had meat at every meal or that it was the man's job to take out the trash. I grew up expecting my future husband to give the forecast, just as my dad did. My dad was a landscaper, and he let us know every morning what the weather would be. I just assumed Stephen would take over this role. Unspoken expectations and unmet needs can lead to discontent and frustration.

At the end of May, I realized we had a month until our wedding in New York!

"Stephen, once we are married, how long does it take the paperwork to be processed?"

"I don't know… maybe a few weeks, maybe a month? Why?"

"Well does it need to be processed to receive the housing allowance? Remember, those apartments aren't going to rent to us until we have all that done."

"Yes, you're right. And the apartments fill up quick around here, especially since it will be summer, and there will be a lot of soldiers changing stations."

Stephen was living in Sam's basement, but we knew that was temporary situation. And Stephen was right. There was always an influx of soldiers changing their duty stations in the summer and competing for the limited housing available. Where would we live?

Paperwork

"I doubt Chaplain Eagle will care once we are married. Even if it takes a week, he won't let me stay there, and to be honest, I kind of feel like I am waiting for him to kick me out at any time."

"Well, what if we get our marriage license sooner?"

A lump formed in my throat. It wasn't what I envisioned. I always imagined signing the papers after the ceremony, with Pastor Bill and the two witnesses signing the marriage certificate as well, beaming with joy.

"I don't know. I want to have our ceremony, and I want to have my dad walk me down the aisle. I have been thinking of how my wedding would be since I was little girl."

"I understand love, but we can still have the ceremony, and that can be our official wedding date, but this can be a formality for the paperwork."

My body felt tingly. I was going to officially be married to the man I love, maybe sooner than I had thought!

"Okay, but let's not tell all our family and friends because I want them to be excited for us, not disappointed that it isn't the traditional wedding."

Alaskan residents can legally officiate weddings with no training or requirements besides residency. We just needed to apply for our license. We went down to the courthouse and received our marriage license within a couple of weeks. There are not too many courthouses, and most of Alaska is rural. Sometimes, people trekked from tiny towns to

Fairbanks to do their big grocery shopping trips. It took them hours to do so. Stephen told Sergeant Drum what we were doing and found out Sergeant Drum was an Alaskan resident. Instead of coordinating for an officiant, he could just sign it.

"Will you help us out, Sergeant Drum?"

Sergeant Drum tapped on the top of the desk.

"I really believe in marriage, and you guys are serious, right? Don't make me regret this!"

So, there in my office, on top of my admin desk, we all signed the marriage license. We were officially husband and wife! I ran, jumped up and down, and hugged Stephen hard. I didn't kiss him right then because I thought that was awkward to do in front of Stephen's soon-to-be supervisor.

With our marriage license signed, we decided we needed to waste no time in getting our tedious paperwork process done for the Army and turned in. We held hands in the car on the way to the administrative building. As soon as he put the car in park, I reached over and kissed my husband. We made our way into the lobby, trying to decipher which room was the correct room to start the process. We had to go to finance. We had to fill out a change of last name for me. We had to fill out paperwork, so the Army could try to station us together if either of us were to come up on new orders to a different duty station. My face shone with pride.

"I cannot believe we are officially married!"

In the Army, there are rules about showing displays of affection when in uniform, but I stood next to Stephen so closely that our

Paperwork

arms touched, and I grabbed his hand, kissed it, and quickly put it back down.

As we finished up and checked off the list, I noticed, out of the corner of my eye, my Caribbean ex-boyfriend.

I turned my back to him and whispered, "Don't see me. Don't see me. Don't see me."

Stephen asked me, "Who are you talking to?"

"Shh… not so loud! It's Cypress," I said through my teeth.

Before he could respond again, I felt a tap on my shoulder; I spun around, and there he was. He was much shorter than I remember, and that smile that once had been charming now looked like the Cheshire cat from Alice in Wonderland.

"Wow, look who it is! Long time, no see. So, what's new?"

"Well, we just got married, and this is my husband."

Wow! That was the first time I said it out loud! It felt good to say those words. I was blessed with a wonderful guy, and he loved me, and I was his number one. I looked up at Stephen and beamed.

"Oh, congratulations. You look good. It's nice to see you. You know, since you're married now, and I'm married…" he turned to Stephen and continued, "to show no hard feelings, I'm having a barbecue, and you should come."

He scribbled his address on a paper and slapped it in my hand.

"So, will we see you later? It will be fun."

"Um… we are busy."

"But, I haven't even told you the time. It's at six."

"Yeah, okay. We gotta go. Bye."

As we rounded the corner to the stairwell, Stephen said to me, "We are not going."

I nodded my head.

"Yeah, I didn't want to go."

Stephen looked down at me.

"Besides, we are newlyweds. I can think of a few things we can do that are way more exhilarating…"

He winked at me and pulled me in close. I giggled, as my face flushed.

Paperwork

In the following weeks, our marriage was official, and we were able to get an apartment. We went back to the same apartment and provided the paperwork to show our marriage. We were approved for an apartment. It was on the third floor, up three flights of stairs, as there was no elevator, and it was our little corner of the world. It was a safe haven, a safe space for us to gather, to invite our friends over and to have a taste of freedom. People no longer could show up on our off time to have us doing all sorts of tasks. My dearest Chaplain Sword and his wife, helped us by gifting us a pot and pan set and gave us one of their pullout couches and a dining set. My mom had a housewarming party in a box and sent me stuff from family and friends in New York. My friends from work and the chapel threw me a bridal shower. I felt as if God gave me these glimmers of light and as if he hugged me through the arms of these women. Many times, when God has spoken into my life, it hasn't been directly; it's been through others. They were my family. They were for us, not against us. They loved me, and they loved Stephen, as they laughed, wept, and shared in our joys and struggles.

Chapter 27

Wedding Invite Fright

We wanted a smaller wedding, and it had to be affordable for our budget at twenty-one and twenty-four years old. We couldn't afford a destination wedding, but I wanted both our families to be there. Texas and New York are worlds apart. I had envisioned my dad walking me down the aisle among family and friends, and Stephen was not sure who could come from his family, so Stephen agreed on a wedding in my hometown.

Our wedding party included my sister and maid of honor, Lianne, and two bridesmaids, my best friend, Savannah, and soon-to-be sister-in-law, Brenita. Stephen's childhood friend, Arthur, was to be the best man, and my uncle, AJ, was his groomsmen. He had also asked his Army buddy, Sam, but his family couldn't make the trip to New York, so he couldn't be in our wedding party.

In February, I called my family and put my mom and sister in

Wedding Invite Fright

charge of helping be my feet on the ground, to put deposits down and pick out everything. I needed decorations and a cake, and my aunt Lisa was going to help with baking cupcakes. My mom helped me book a photographer. Check. Put a deposit down on a venue. Check. My mom searched for wedding ceremony venues, and since I had grown up there, my mom checked with the pastor, and he let us hold the ceremony there for free. Check.

My grandmother worked for a print company and offered to help with the invitations and pay for them, and she sent me samples of silver letters, one with blue roses that matched the bridesmaid's dresses. I thought red, white, and blue were the perfect colors because we were in the military. We had the bouquets made with red and white flowers, with touches of blue. My uncle, AJ, who was more like a brother to me, was in our wedding party and also was in the Air Force. He would wear his dress blues. My husband would wear his uniform, which was green, and Arthur, Stephen's best friend from childhood, would wear his Navy uniform that was a different color blue. For the bridesmaids' dresses, I settled on a periwinkle blue with a satin finish. My mom's best friend helped with the decorations, and she also was a seamstress, so she graciously offered to alter my dress and make a veil and flowers.

My mom and dad helped by giving us some money for the DJ and putting down a deposit on the Italian restaurant where the reception was going to be held. My mom actually did more planning than I did. I was grateful. My mom ran things by me, but frankly, with all that was going on in the Army with us, I felt as if I had little time to devote to planning a wedding in six short months. We (with my mom's, sister's, and friend's ideas and execution) decorated ourselves, and we crafted, enlisting the help of my mom's friends and my friends to make the cute goodie bag gifts and flowers made of Hershey's kisses and green stems. Our family friend, Sue, made the alterations to my dress, made my veil, and made the floral arrangements for my bridesmaids, along with my bouquet. It was tasteful, but we were operating on a low budget.

The invitations officially went out in February. Since we were all the way in Alaska, I knew that a lot of our friends wouldn't be able to attend our wedding all the way across the U.S., but I thought I would send one to those closest to us, for the sentiment and to let them know we wished they could attend if it was possible, and we loved them. I thought nothing of the fact that I sent the invitations to many chaplains and chaplain assistant families that had been like my second family, but not to Chaplain Eagle, who didn't approve of our relationship. A week after our wedding, Chaplain Eagle called my husband to come to his office. We knew something was going to happen because we had gotten back from leave, and he had promised to have a "serious discussion" once we had returned from leave.

He said he needed to talk to Stephen now and then had Stephen sit in the waiting area of his office for an hour. For the appointment Chaplain Eagle had set, Stephen sat sixty agonizing minutes, while the office administrator, Ms. Clark, went back and forth, perplexed and questioning why Chaplain Eagle had him waiting. Ms. Clark told her boss when Stephen arrived and told Stephen there was nothing else happening, that he was not busy, so she was confused why he wasn't seeing him. Finally, Ms. Clark let him in.

Chaplain Eagle didn't turn around or acknowledge Stephen's presence for twenty additional minutes. He nonchalantly typed and checked email at his desk with his back toward Stephen. Stephen had to stand at attention, which means he faced forward, silently waiting, as is customary in an officer's presence until called at ease. Finally, Chaplain Eagle rose from his desk, turned, and stepped to the front.

Wedding Invite Fright

"At ease, Specialist Hayes. Have a seat in here."

He closed the door and then sat back in his chair. He scooted his chair two inches from Stephen and rose up his chair with the lever on the side, until he was looking down at Stephen. He sat looking at him for a minute in silence until Stephen spoke up.

"You wanted to see me, sir?"

"Yes. I am very hurt and disappointed."

"Sir?"

"Yes. Why wasn't I invited to your wedding? Don't you like me?"

Stephen paused, taking a breath. He needed to choose his words carefully. He had to tell the truth or lie to a field grade officer, which is a punishable offense.

"With all due respect, sir, why would I send you an invitation? Sir, you don't like me, and frankly, sir, I don't care for you either."

Chaplain Eagle's gray eyebrows danced up and down his face, eyes widening at Stephen's candor, as he still hovered above. His mouth kept opening and closing, not sure what to say next.

"What?!? I-I-I don't not like you!"

"Sir, since I've been here, I have carried a lot of weight, and you keep piling it on. I just get it done. You have treated me poorly and don't like my relationship with Specialist Whiteman. Sir, we don't have to like each other. We just have to work together for the soldiers, and since I've been here, I have done nothing but that, sir."

Chaplain Eagle dismissed him. Stephen called me after he left his office.

"You told him you didn't like him?"

"Well, I couldn't lie. He was already looking for ways to discredit me and punish me. At least I don't have to see him as often."

That was the last one-on-one interaction Stephen would have to face with Chaplain Eagle. Stephen still had to work with him on occasion when everyone was together, but at least now he was officially in a new unit with a new chain of command. Stephen was promoted shortly after being integrated to his new unit. The brigade chaplain and sergeant, as well as his unit, recognized his work ethic, attention to detail, and his care for the soldiers. Stephen met the required qualifications, and the unit set a day for his promotion ceremony. Stephen asked me to pin on his rank; I was honored with his request.

It was a windy and chilly spring day. The ground was wet, as spring break up was known to be there, and the mounds of snow that Alaskan winter had brought were dwindling down. Scattered puddles and half melted snow patches surrounded his unit's area. I strategically stepped around, as I made it to the back corner of the formation. I felt honored to share this moment. I admired Stephen, as I stood at attention in the back of his company of soldiers. Stephen seemed to hold ambition in one hand and respect in the other. The way he confronted problems in a bold manner, yet showing consideration, inspired me. He was finally getting what he deserved. No, not what he deserved—what he had earned.

His first sergeant read his orders, "Know Ye, that reposing special trust and confidence in the fidelity and abilities of Stephen Hayes, Jr., I do promote him to sergeant in the United States Army."

That was my cue to make my way to the front, to pin on Stephen's sergeant rank. I stepped back, right faced, and jogged up toward him. The Army calls that moving with a purpose, and walking was not going to cut it. I needed to move fast. As I rounded the front column of soldiers, my foot slid, and my eyes bulged. I was going down. A small cry escaped from my lips, as I landed on my back on a small patch of black ice. Right in front of the whole formation, I wiped out. Chuckles echoed from the rows of infantrymen, despite being at attention. Stephen tried to hold his composure, eyes straight forward, but I saw his face fight off a smile. I popped up as a warm red glow crossed my ears and face. I placed the insignia on his chest and gave it a punch. (In the old Army days, the pins stabbed the soldiers, but in recent days, it's been a Velcro insignia, so soldiers get the rank and a punch on top of the rank placed onto the chest.)

When at attention, eyes should be forward, the face solemn, arms at your sides with hands closed, and feet together at a forty-five-degree angle. I don't think I could be as gracious, seeing me fall, but Stephen always reminded me, by example, to be professional and do the right thing.

Once his sergeant rank was "pinned," everyone was able to come forward to congratulate Stephen. I grabbed him, pressing my body against his.

"You didn't help me up!" I chastised him. "I kind of hate and admire that." I smirked.

"Sorry, love, but I had to abide by military regulations."

Of course he did. I was mostly joking. Stephen was on to better things, and I felt a twinge in my chest. I wouldn't have him working with me by my side, and I wouldn't have the protection of his knowledge and his strength to fight against what was wrong. I pushed those thought backs. Regardless of our physical proximity, I knew Stephen would always be there for support, and shortly, he would be my forever support as my husband.

Chapter 28

Wedding Day

Stephen and I stepped off the plane in New York and hit the ground running. Dress rehearsal was Friday, and we put the last minute touches on everything. I figured out the seating, which is a lot of strategic planning that reminded me of chess. I put people with others so they'd get along. You have certain seats of honor where grandparents and parents sit that are closer. It's a whole thing, and I knew nothing of it and got a crash course in it the night before we said "I do." When my husband's mom, sister, and best friend made it to New York, they spent time with us and my parents at my parent's house before the rehearsal at the church. The night before, we ate one of my dad's favorite takeout foods. It was summer, so my mom had just stockpiled some fruit and had cut up some melons.

After meeting Stephen's family for the first time, my hospitable mom offered our guests some food and drink.

"Are you hungry? We have some fried chicken, some Kool-Aid,

and some watermelon."

"Mom!"

"What?"

"Stop!"

"What?"

"Really? Fried chicken and Kool-Aid?"

Stephen's family erupted in laughter. How could she not know? I'm not sure if they knew it was a joke, or that they were just incredulous at the situation we found ourselves in. Stephen's best friend stopped laughing, looked at mom, and smirked.

"Why? Is it because we are black? You have nothing else, or did you just stock up on black food?"

My mom stammered, "No, no. It's, it's not like that. I swear! It's just what we had in our fridge. I eat watermelon and chicken, and we have Kool-Aid. If you had come a day earlier, it would have been burgers and macaroni salad. Honest!"

Oh, Mom! I thought about the amusing, yet awkward positions Stephen and I have found ourselves in. One time, Stephen and I were invited to a dinner party at a friend's house. After we had eaten all the good food, Stephen realized we should go, as it was getting late. My future husband said thank you and got up from the table.

"Well, you know how we black folk get…"

I interrupted, "No. Tell me how we get?" Everyone erupted in laughter. It was the stereotype that black people eat and run. He sometimes forgets, and I sometimes forget. It's not that we don't know the difference in our skin colors; it's just not something on the forefront of

Wedding Day

our mind at all times.

As I got ready for bed that night, I could barely sleep. I was going to be married to the love of my life. Stephen left with his family to stay the night in the nearby hotel so he would be surprised to see me in my dress on our wedding day.

When my alarm clock beeped, I realized it was finally morning. I am usually not a morning person, but this morning was different. Once I realized what day it, was I sprang up out of bed. I was eager to get ready to marry my sweet fiancé.

My Aunt Lisa helped to tame my thick, wavy, frizzy hair, and my best friend's sister did my makeup. My mom, my Aunt Lisa, and Grandma went dress shopping at the bridal sale, right before I had flown to Dallas on the previous trip. I smiled as I picked up my dress. The wedding dress I picked out was a simple and budget-friendly, strapless white satin dress, with iridescent, beaded ribbon framing the bust and a small slit in the center of the top, with a sweet bow in the front below it. The most beautiful part of my dress, and the reason I chose the dress, was the back. White satin dime-sized buttons spaced every inch all down the back to the medium-sized train. I felt like a princess. Our photographer snapped a couple of photos of me getting ready. As usual, I was running late.

Meanwhile, on the other side of town, Stephen was finished getting ready with his best man, Arthur. They drove over to the church early, in typical Stephen fashion. The church where we held the ceremony was a simple and quaint church in a little town called Loch Sheldrake.

There was a lake behind it that had a pretty view, and the church was the same church I had grown up in. More importantly, it was free for me to use, as my family were active members. It is off a main route, so it gets a bit of traffic flow, especially in the summer when people come up from the city to their summer homes. Stephen put on his blinker to turn, and when he was able, he made a U-turn to park in front of the church because there was only parking on one side of that street. When Stephen and Arthur stood outside the car, they heard a pinging sound. Ping! Ping! Ping!

"What's that?"

They started looking around, and a rock whizzed by their heads. A lady stood on the other side of the street at the gas station, spewing derogatory terms at them, throwing rocks at them. Arthur balled his fists and slid across the front of the car swiftly, but Stephen grabbed his shoulder.

"Hey, let's just go inside. It's my wedding day."

He didn't think it would go over well if he spent our wedding night in jail. He was right. He would have been a dead man. Was it road rage, or was it disdain for their appearance? It seemed clear to me. I have never had someone yell slurs and throw rocks at me before.

Inside, the groomsmen seated our guests, and our wedding party made their way down the aisle.

By the time my bridesmaids and I made it to the church, my stomach felt as if my intestines were twisted and tangled up inside. I thought

Wedding Day

I might pass out from the nerves. I had to pee like a racehorse, and they do not make it easy in a wedding dress. My bridesmaids had to hold up my dress and its train, as I steadied and tried to hover. My future sister-in-law, who had only known me in person for about a week, got on a new closeness level with me in that moment.

My dad paced a bit in the foyer, waiting to see if we were ready. I was late to my own wedding, forty-five minutes late by the time all was said and done. When the music started playing, I thought, This is it. It was time to walk down the aisle to my best friend. My dad smiled down at me, tears brimming in his eyes, and squeezed my hand.

"I love you. Are you ready?"

I almost cried then. Growing up, I could count the number of times I saw a single tear teeter to the edge and roll down his face—once for my graduation, once when sending me off to the Army, and now.

When the double doors swung open, I saw that everyone was standing, but I only searched for one pair of eyes—Stephen's. Stephen's smile was so warm, and he wiped away tears that kept swelling over the brim of his eyelids. I walked toward him, my eyes never leaving his gaze. The wedding photographer flashed lights. Other cameras flickered and flashed. If it had been up to me, I would have skipped down that aisle like a kid at Christmas time.

The photographer tried to take pictures, but I just wanted him to move from the aisle, so I could get up there to my future husband.

Finally, I made it to the front. Pastor Bill, a longtime family friend, stood as the gatekeeper. He beamed.

"Who will give this bride to be married?"

CAMOUFLAGED LOVE

My dad raised his hand.

"My mother and I... Oops, I mean her mother and I."

Chuckles erupted.

Pastor Bill cleared his throat and started the ceremony.

"God is Love, but what is love? First Corinthians thirteen says, 'Love is patient. Love is kind. Love does not envy. It keeps no record of wrongs. It looks for the best.'"

Many times, I thought back to this verse, and I can say Stephen is patient. Stephen is kind. Stephen keeps no record of wrongs. Stephen is the definition of love. He wasn't perfect, but he was perfect for me. He saw me. He knew my flaws and faults, and he still chose me. What a picture of God's redeeming love, in human form!

We lit the unity candle, and I pursed my lips, scared I might light my veil on fire because I accidentally lit a potholder on fire in this same church, at a Valentine's Day dinner previously. Luckily, no firefighters needed to be called for this wedding. Pastor Bill cleared his throat and explained the significance of the unity candle.

"A cord of three strands is not easily broken." The two of us, with God in the middle, would be a potent force.

"Do you, Lorin, take Stephen to have and to hold, for richer or poor, in sickness and in health?" Oh, it's quiet. Wait, what? I had forgotten my cue in this part of our vows because I was gazing at my soon-to-be husband's eyes and smiling. Pastor Bill cleared his throat and then

Wedding Day

whispered.

"That's where you answer 'I do,' if you do."

"Ah, sorry. Yes. I mean, yes, I do."

Stephen looked relieved, as the sweat on his brow glistened. Pastor Bill continued, "People only seem to want to marry for the health and richer parts, but during life, there are ups and downs. It doesn't say for better and only better, or for only when things are good, or when your body is a perfect ten. It's through thick and thin, through sickness and hospital visits, through storms of this life."

I nodded. I still felt as if I was up in the sky, walking on the clouds.

It was as if I was floating above, yet there in the moment as well. I saw my soon-to-be husband, using his hand to wipe a few tears that escaped his eye, and my sister-in-law and best friend both crying in my peripheral vision.

I felt as if I was going to burst out of my skin. I heard Pastor Bill say, "You may now kiss the bride." We kissed, a respectable kiss, a "PG-13" kiss.

"I now pronounce you husband and wife. For the very first time, Mr. and Mrs. Stephen Hayes!"

I stuck my bouquet up in the air, held our hands up in triumph, and was flooded with emotions. The whole room cheered.

We had the best time at our reception. I danced my shoes off. I love dancing. Stephen and I danced to Michael Jackson's "Thriller." Then, Stephen persuaded my grandma to dance with him on the floor! We danced our first dance as husband and wife to Lifehouse: "It's you and me, and all other people. I don't know why I can't take my eyes off of you!"

We did the "Cha-cha slide", and I glanced around at family and friends who were celebrating us being together. The restaurant workers even joined in on the Conga line. They said they had never had such a fun reception. Sure, they might have said that to every wedding party, but our family knows how to have a good time, and I like to tell myself it's because it was the best wedding ever. I didn't want the night to end.

We said goodbye to our guests, and we left for hotel nearby. When we went out to the car, there were a bunch of cans tied on strings to the end, and some friends and family had decorated our car with magnets saying "Just married," and "Mr. & Mrs. Happily Ever After." We drove to our hotel. As we got out, my husband offered his hand. I wrestled with my dress, trying to not flash anyone as teen onlookers hooted, whistled, and clapped loudly.

"Woo! We know what you're doing here!"

"All night long! Woo woo!"

Ugh.

I burrowed my red face in Stephen's arm. It's weird to know that everyone knows what happens on your wedding night. This was not dinner and a show, people! I grabbed Stephen's hand and hurried inside the hotel lobby. After we got the key, we held hands down the hallway to our room. He picked me up and carried me over the threshold. It was just like every single romantic movie I had ever watched, magical. I squealed in delight and tilted my head back, bumping my head on the doorframe.

"Ouch! That's gonna leave a mark."

We laughed, as he closed the door.

Chapter 29

Back Up

Being married to Stephen was blissful. The first year was not as easy as one might think because we still had the tension of Chaplain Eagle, but now we knew they couldn't take legal action against our relationship. I saw Church, Fox, and Waters attend different trainings to advance their careers, and I thought I wanted to stay in, so I asked about going to some of the trainings, too. Maybe if I could become a funds clerk, I wouldn't have to be near Chaplain Eagle's eyes, or maybe if I could go to leadership training, I would be able to do something new. At least I would have the rank to feel a little more established, almost as if to say, "Here I am. I am here to stay. You didn't win." I brought those requests to Sergeant Church. I had to go through the chain of command, of course, as is expected in the Army.

"Sorry, Specialist Hayes. Chaplain Eagle says we need someone responsible to take care of the chapels and all these duties, and you're it." I watched bitterly, as they took turns and went to several trainings, and I filled in for their positions a few ranks above my own. Specialist Fox went to leadership training and became a sergeant. I was tasked with some of his obligations because "we know you are responsible," which made me confused. If I was of good quality, enough to be able to be recommended for a promotion, how was I not responsible enough? Sergeant Church presented me with a few Army achievement medals for my work, so maybe things were turning around? If I was going through all these things and working so hard, maybe I could be promoted too. At least I would be better compensated for my work. I could try to get ready, so when I could be sent off to training, I would have what I needed to be promoted. Maybe I could get this done. Maybe I could be promoted. Stephen made me feel confident. He had gone over to the infantry division and was promoted within a few months. He earned that promotion, but I started to feel a twinge of jealousy. I wanted to be respected by my peers, to be seen as valuable and someone who was the leader I had so desperately needed. He encouraged me to grow. At home, I worked on studying for the board exam with him, and I continued to do so, on my own. I kept taking classes and online trainings to try to bring my promotion points up.

Working through these challenges, now the only female in my unit, made me feel lonely. At least when Stephen was there, I had someone who had my back. I didn't always think the other soldiers were against me, but I had seen that they weren't necessarily for me, and at the least, they were terrified of pissing off Chaplain Eagle.

I tried to have lunch with Stephen a few times a week at least.

Back Up

Then I got to be away from anyone who made me work through my lunch. I came over and unloaded on him daily. He gave me advice and helped me balance between sticking up for myself and forgiveness. Stephen took his time before speaking to me, acknowledging my pain and my process, but always pushing me to do better.

About four months into our marriage, Sergeant Church told me that things would ease up a little soon because we were getting a new soldier, Sergeant Carr, who would be there soon.

I did a cartwheel in my mind. This was going to be great. I would have someone in my corner. For a minute, I felt a lump in my throat. I mean, Sergeant Tiger didn't exactly work out for me, but this was a different person, and I needed to give her the benefit of the doubt, so I pushed those thoughts aside.

Sergeant Carr felt the tension and vibes between the other people in our unit and me, so I told her an abridged version of some of what had happened. She listened and nodded, and I thought she really understood me. She was a female, so she must have been through some of this stuff!

She filled in being the sergeant in charge of the chapel. She essentially filled the shoes of Stephen. She quickly decided she wanted my job instead of manning the front desk at the counseling center. Even though I still mowed the lawns and all that, she decided to send me back to manage the chapel and take my job.

"You have it too cushy over here. You do what you want because no one is over here, don't you?"

"Sergeant?"

"You come and go, and they don't know where you are half the time, so you are going to need to check in with me all the time."

No! God, please give me a break! I guess here we go again. I hated being micromanaged. She didn't see me because there are a zillion and one things to do, and I was always running.

"Hooah, Sergeant." Hooah is what we say in the Army. It means yes, and it means agreement, but sometimes it is said because it's obligatory, and this was how a lot of our conversations went.

A few months in, I decided to get a manicure. I used to get them done with Kelly, but it had been awhile, and I wanted to do something to relax. I showed up to work, chipper and ready to start the day. I went to the counseling center with some paperwork for Sergeant Carr.

She grabbed my hand and pulled it closer.

I knew my nails looked amazing.

"And what is that on your fingers?"

Oh, she's not kidding. I straightened my face. "Sergeant, do you mean my nail polish? I think it's called an American manicure?"

Back Up

"You cannot have two different colors. Take those off now."

"Sergeant, it's not two different colors. It's my nail color and the white tip."

"You have until the end of the day to get those removed."

"So, I have to tear off my fingernails, Sergeant?"

"You too prissy for hard work?"

"No, Sergeant."

"Why do you have on makeup everyday anyways? You're just going to sweat it off."

"Sergeant, it's within regulations."

"I'm going to find out about that because I don't think you can do all these things. I think you are taking advantage of being the only female. Fix that hair."

"Hooah, Sergeant."

My hair looked crazy because I had just finished raking outside, my face was sweaty, and all my baby hairs were sticking up. This continued to be the tone of our encounters, her telling me to get myself together, that I was being too prissy, and rolling her eyes at me. Sergeant Carr judged me for everything I was and everything I did. I'm not sure why. Maybe it was because I wasn't an airborne soldier like her? Maybe it was because we were complete opposites? I wore makeup everyday in uniform because it made me feel good. Sometimes when I looked good, I felt better Maybe it was because women feel as if they have to compete, that there was only room for one token female in a male-dominated space. I didn't believe that, but I could feel that she didn't like to be compared to me, and I didn't like to be compared to her. I didn't really want to be the "alpha." I just wanted to be a part of a pack. As the days went on, I almost wished I could be dealing with Sergeant Church again. At least he seemed not to nitpick at my appearance. At least he didn't make me do flutter kicks and pushups all the time. I was over it. I felt as if I couldn't do anything to please her. Truth be told, my nails were fine, but the regulations are ambiguous when it comes to certain things, and nails and hair cannot be "faddish." It is up to the commander's discretion, so Sergeant Church probably figured as a female, she knew better, so he stayed out of it.

Sergeant Carr came next door one day to give me an earful.

"Sergeant Church is an idiot. I don't want to deal with his nonsense, and he needs someone to go do to the chaplain's office and do official mail and pick up a box of Bibles. I'm sending you, since you don't seem like you're busy, as you have time to do whatever and not answer the chapel phone. Where were you?"

"Sergeant, I have been at the chapel all day! I don't know when you called, but I was cleaning, and the phone doesn't ring back near the sacristy or storage room."

"I came in through the back. You weren't there when I came over five minutes ago."

I was indignant. I rolled my eyes. "I just went to the bathroom.

Back Up

Sergeant, my car is literally outside."

"You have an excuse for everything, don't you? Drop and give me twenty."

At least I was a beast at doing pushups.

Sergeant Carr wrote me a counseling statement about being where I was supposed to be, and I had to start checking in every hour by phone. I had to begin emailing everyone in my unit daily about what I had going on, so I could cover my back with a paper trail. They were annoyed. I copied them on every email, but it was my evidence of what was going on.

"Sergeant, I sent an email of my tasks I did today, so you would know where I had to go."

Sergeant Carr didn't like me, but funny enough, she loved Stephen. Whenever he came around, she was so nice to him, inviting him to share a beer with her and her husband sometime. Even though she was hard on me and didn't like me, unlike her male counterparts, she never commented about my relationship with Stephen or my period, which was a relief. Also, in time, I realized that the very thing she was accusing me of, skirting work and leaving early, was her custom.

All the while, I fought an internal battle. I found that the worthiness issue at work was creeping in harder, but the pain of the rape and trauma also reared its ugly head. All throughout dating, it was there, and it affected me, but I pushed it down, deep within my body. I could not deal with it, but now we were married, and I thought it would just dissipate and float away like the clouds. Instead of worrying and focusing on our relationship and not getting in trouble, I couldn't see my way past my trauma. It bubbled up within me.

When Stephen closed the door too quickly behind me, I began to shake and sob. If he came up behind me to put his arms around me, I yelled, and then even though I realized it was him, I had a panic attack. I never told anyone about this. I didn't know what it was at the time. I had pushed that trauma deep within. When Stephen kissed my neck, if he touched my leg unexpectedly, sometimes any movement of him advancing toward me triggered me, tears sprang up suddenly, like a hurricane, rattling my entire body, chest concaving with a throbbing feeling that I thought I might die.

Stephen wasn't forceful. He stopped in those moments. He asked what he could do to help. Sometimes that was holding my hand. Sometimes that was a hug. Many times it was prayer. Guilt made me feel that it wasn't fair for Stephen to weather this. He wasn't the one who crashed the gate of my boundaries, but he was the one who was there to deal with the aftermath.

"I'm sorry. I know it's not your fault. You didn't sign up for this. I wouldn't blame you if you don't want to deal with me." Stephen took my hands in his.

"I love you. I married you. I married all of you—the good and the hard times too. I don't regret it, and I will do whatever I have to do to help you, to trust me, and show you that I love you."

I started regularly sitting in and learning at the Bible studies and functions that I also worked at each week. Battling my inner struggles, I sat down and heard Chaplain Staff's wife, Liza, share about worth and how God sees me as a beloved daughter. Another chaplain's wife, Jackie, also breathed life into me. She helped me see that I needed to extend the grace I gave toward others, to myself. God used many of the women, and some of the chaplain assistants and chaplains who were imperfect but loving people, to begin the process of healing from the church hurt.

In Japanese art, they have something called Kintsugi, where they take broken pottery and lacquer the pieces back together with silver or gold. All those cracks, all those imperfections, are made into the most beautiful and unique designs. Once broken and now whole, unique and more beautiful than before. Kintsugi was me. God was the potter, and he was taking all these broken pieces and making me into someone worth celebrating.

Chapter 30

To Reenlist or Not Reenlist?

Stephen's unit came closer to the looming deployment to Iraq. We only had a rough estimate of the timeline when they were deploying. I prayed about it and considered that since Stephen was going to deploy with the brigade, I should too. I was coming up on the end of my Army contract with four months to go and was told I had to reenlist to have enough time to deploy.

I talked to the retention sergeant about how to make sure that I was moved from my current unit. I was over the work situation, and there was no way I wanted to get stuck in the same environment for another three to six years. Sergeant Church and Sergeant Carr said Chaplain Eagle could help work it out to trade personnel, if I just reenlisted first.

Stephen warned me.

To Reenlist or Not Reenlist?

"Sign nothing, unless they write you pinpoint orders to a unit in the brigade; they legally don't have to help you move or approve your move to another unit and then you will be stuck where you are."

I talked to the brigade sergeant and chaplain. They were on board with me moving over to the brigade. There was an incoming soldier for the slot I wanted, but he had just gotten back from a deployment, so he agreed to take some time with his family, as he had been away for twelve months. He was grateful that I could switch with him.

My unit was frustrated with me. They needed to know numbers and were understaffed for the amount of work there was, even though technically, there weren't any open job slots in the garrison to fill. They hounded me daily to know my decision. I remained firm.

"Sergeant, I will reenlist if I can get pinpoint orders in my contract."

Several weeks went by, and my husband called me and asked if I was at the chapel. I was excited! This was it. I was going to be out of here!

I was mopping the floors when he and Sergeant Drum showed up.

I put the mop in the bucket and greeted them at the door, and he asked to go talk in my office. My husband and Sergeant Drum followed me there. I shut the door and felt the weight of the moment, even before he said a word. From the looks on their faces, the news wasn't good. Sergeant Drum looked uneasy as he took a breath.

"I have some news. Unfortunately, it was not the news I wanted to give. It came down the pipeline that Chaplain Eagle tried to get the incoming chaplain assistant, the one you were going to switch with, into garrison, and he was also planning on keeping you at the chapel."

My lungs felt like a deflated balloon that you let go of. All the air had been sucked out. and I was blowing back and forth. He paused and gave me sympathetic eyes and then continued.

"A colonel in the brigade got wind of this shady dealing, so now that incoming chaplain assistant has pinpoint assignment orders to that line unit."

I paced back in forth in front of him, seething.

"Are you kidding me, Sergeant? How can he do that? Isn't there anything that can be done? Can he still switch once he's here?"

"I'm afraid not. You can't get out of these orders. There is no wiggle room. I tried everything I could, and even Chaplain Staff tried what he could. I'm sorry to disappoint you."

My eyes brimmed with tears. "Sergeant, I understand it's not your fault. I'm furious, but it's not at you. Thank you for at least trying for me."

How can one person ruin or meddle so much in my life and major decisions? This was unfair. This was a low blow. Why was there always

To Reenlist or Not Reenlist?

something?

Stephen hugged me.

"Sorry, love. I love you."

I let tears trickle down my cheeks, down my chin, and onto his uniform. After a minute, he lifted my head and cupped my face, looking straight into my eyes.

"It's not like this everywhere. Don't let one bad experience stop you if you want to stay in the Army. You are a good soldier. You care, and that's what we need. We need soldiers who care, ones who will become leaders who care."

I pondered that, but I was stuck. I could reenlist for another assignment in a different place while Stephen was deployed, but I could be deployed separately, or we could be separated for years at different bases. What then? The Army "tries" to keep you together, but there's no guarantee. It's mission first. After praying and discussing this with my mentors and mulling it over with Stephen, I made my decision; I was breaking up with the Army. I turned in my discharge paperwork and leave form. I had enough leave (vacation time) saved up for the beginning of July through September, and we were in June, so there was fewer than a few weeks to go.

Once Sergeant Carr realized that me getting out meant she was going to be flying solo and doing everything I was doing at both areas of operation, without an incoming soldier, she changed tactics.

"Hey, I know you wanted to go to the leadership course, or is there another training you want to do? I'm sure I can get you in there, no problem."

"No thanks, Sergeant."

She sweetly asked if I could cash in at least some of my leave because she was going to be swamped.

"I could really use you. You are a hard worker. It's going to be just me. Holy crap! You have a lot of leave saved up! You know you could cash some of that in, and that would help you and me."

Wait. After months of commenting on how inept I was, how I was not being a good soldier and was getting out of work, and not doing my job, now I am a hard worker? I looked into it and found out she was right. I could cash out my leave, but I would get paid much less after taxes than if I just stayed in and went on vacation, receiving my regular pay for the last three months.

Sergeant Carr knew that I cared about my character and didn't want to be known as a blue falcon (a soldier who screws over a buddy). I realized it was more of a convenience and not because she really cared. I had mixed feelings because I didn't want my character to be twisted or tainted, but I also didn't want to stay a day longer than necessary.

To Reenlist or Not Reenlist?

"Well, we could just get your contract extended and send you to school anyway, whether you like it or not."

"Sergeant, I will not go."

"You'll have to go. It will be a direct order."

"Sergeant, then I won't pass my class, so they will send me back."

I was stubborn, and even though I knew how to follow orders, I wasn't backing down this time.

"If you purposefully fail out of school, then you can get an Article 15, and I will see to it that you get a dishonorable discharge. That will make it hard for you to get any job."

A dishonorable discharge is such a big deal because as soon as employers see military service on a resume, they know to ask for the discharge papers. It's nearly impossible to get a job or receive veteran benefits without an honorable discharge. It could literally ruin your life, your career, aspirations, or cause loss of military benefits, such as the GI Bill for paid college tuition, insurance, and other benefits. Later, I realized these were scare tactics, as the Army would not send a soldier to school with only a few months remaining. It would be a waste of money, so they wouldn't do it. It would not be up to Sergeant Carr to extend my contract. The Army could do that, but it would have to be from further up the chain of command and for a specific reason, like medical treatment or deployment.

This time, I didn't wait for anymore escalation. I went and talked directly to my sergeant major.

"Sergeant Major, I am getting out." My voice felt strangely strong to me. This can't be my voice, but it is!

"Sergeant Major Swamp, I appreciate all your mentorship and all your help." I paused, pushing the lump down in my throat. "I know Sergeant Carr, and maybe the others in the unit, want me to go to school, but I don't see the point because I don't plan on continuing in the Army. I am ready to leave."

"I understand. And you are sure I can't change your mind? You have a good head on your shoulders. I hate to see you leave this way." I shook my head.

"Sergeant Major, I'm sure."

"Okay, I will support you in what you want to do. Do you have a job lined up? Don't get out without a plan. Do you know what you will do?"

"I will finish up my degree, and I have some prospective jobs. I don't know what I will need. Well, actually, would it be okay to give your information if they ask for a professional reference? I don't think anyone else will be a help there."

"Sure, and I can write you a letter of recommendation if you would like."

To Reenlist or Not Reenlist?

"Thank you, Sergeant Major. That means a lot to me."

I could tell he was a little disappointed because he thought I would reenlist, but he supported me and gave that space for me to make my own choice. He wrote me a letter of recommendation for any potential future jobs, as a character reference. I felt lighter than I had in years

As I left his office, my phone registered all the calls from Sergeant Carr that I let go to voicemail while in my meeting. I told her I had errands to do earlier but not where I would be, partly because I didn't want her interfering, and it had been on the way to another appointment I had to go to for chapel business. I stepped out of Sergeant Major Swamp's office and sighed. Here goes nothing. I had to call her back. She answered before the first ring ended.

"Where the hell are you? You trying to get out of work again? You never pick up the chapel phone when I call!" I rolled my eyes.

"Sergeant, I do when I am in my office, but if I am working outside or going to the main chaplain office or all these other things, I don't answer it. I emailed you to let you know where I was going to be!"

"You have a craploaded of things to do, and you are slacking. Get back here now!"

My eyes flashed. Did my coworkers want me to end up on the six o'clock news? I could see it now: "Stressed Soldier Charged with Choking Supervisor."

In the last month, I felt the pressure and tension bubbling over. I had to be careful to be early to things because if I was late, I knew that she was looking for any excuse to stick it to me. It felt as though she wanted to break me. Don't get yourself in trouble and lose your benefits. Just put your nose to the grindstone. I could see that light at the end of the tunnel.

The last days of my work at the chapel, being under Sergeant Carr's thumb, were drawing to an end, and I could taste the freedom. Finally, there was one last work day to go before I had to do the out-processing steps. How bad could it be?

Sergeant Carr multiplied the manual labor for that last week, but the last day, she decided I should mow the lawn and weed it again, wipe down every glass door, and sweep and mop every floor. This was a part of my job, but they had already been completed. I was as hot as a tea kettle inside, but I combated my feelings by singing praise and worship songs as I worked.

"Hayes, are you finished with your tasks?"

"Yes, Sergeant."

"Tell me then, what is this is in the rock bed?"

"Grass, Sergeant."

To Reenlist or Not Reenlist?

"Well, it looks terrible. You need to fix it."

"Hooah, Sergeant. I'll use the blower."

Her grin plastered across her face in amusement.

"No, you won't. You need to pick every blade of grass out by hand, or you are not finished for the day. Until you are officially out, you are still a soldier, and you have follow orders of a commanding officer. I don't care how long it takes."

If I was a cartoon, steam would have flowed from my ears. God gave me supernatural self-control because I wanted to lunge at her. A few months ago, I would have cried because I was so angry, but I refused her the satisfaction. I could have used the blower, and it would be done quickly, but this was revenge and punishment. I clenched my jaw.

"Hooah, Sergeant."

Nervousness and relief washed over me, as I reached being ten days away from hanging up my uniform for good. I had the arduous task of out-processing in ten days' time. This process, when done properly, normally takes weeks to months, depending on the soldier, but you can start the out-processing within the year to set yourself up for life outside the Army. I had to clean and turn in my TA-50 Army supplies and things handed to me upon arrival, such as snow gear, canteens, ponchos, vortex, and gloves. I had to rush around to all the buildings on post to have them check off dental and doctors' records, all the important documentation on post to make sure I didn't have any overdue library books, and I didn't rent a tent, bikes, or RVs from outdoor recreational department. I stopped at the military police station to make sure I didn't have any outstanding speeding tickets. I turned in my hospital ID I had used to serve at the hospital's chapel, finished the paperwork, took some outgoing classes on reintegrating into society, resume building, gaining federal employment, and how to market my skill set to the outside civilian world. Information was overloaded with logistics of where my household goods were going to be shipped and what my next steps were. I should have a plan getting out. Yes! My spirit felt like doing donuts inside, but at the same time, I felt a little like my air had been let out of my tires. I had not mentally prepared myself to leave the Army.

    I wanted to feel free, and a surge ran through my body at the prospect that I could speak my mind without consequence. I don't have to use formalities. I can tell these leaders exactly what I thought of them! I had a plan to wait until I was completely out, so no harm could befall me. I had every intention of marching back to their offices and telling them off, but that small voice told me not to. The flames of retaliation and the fire of contempt began to flicker. I had conviction. That was not the kind of person I was or who I wanted to be. All that rage, that vengeful spirit and resentment, wasn't healthy. That wasn't going to make things right. Nelson Mandela once said, "Resentment is like drinking poison and then hoping it will kill your enemies."

    I had to ask God to help work in me with my anger because I was enraged enough to hurt them with the fiercest and sharpest weapon I had, my tongue. But what would that accomplish? They would win, and I would lose. That was giving them too much power. I could give them a piece of my mind, but at the cost of giving them my peace. A piece for peace? It wasn't worth it. I couldn't do that. That wasn't for me.

To Reenlist or Not Reenlist?

Instead, I told myself that I needed the poise of a queen, the heart of Mother Teresa, and the forgiving spirit of Nelson Mandela. I thought about the one person who encapsulated the good qualities of all those individuals I look up to, who died at the hands of others and still chose to say, "Forgive them father, for they know not what they do." That was Jesus.

People act out in a way because they convince themselves of something, but if they truly had an understanding of what love is and what truth is, they wouldn't continue doing hurtful things. Or maybe they wouldn't care. It's possible they understood their actions were ugly and, even more, why they were ugly, but they were determined to act out anyway. Whatever the case, I knew I had to bite my tongue and just get through this one last thing. The last formality was the Hail and Farewell. Surely, if others who had been hurt much worse could forgive their captives for far more, I could forgive mine.

Chapter 31

Farewells & Forgiveness

Hail and Farewells are celebrations to both welcome incoming soldiers and say goodbye and send off soldiers moving on to their next duty stations. They are also used when soldiers retire or decide to not reenlist. The honorees get to pick a favorite restaurant where it's held and get presented with awards, acknowledgements, and appreciation for all their hard work. Sometimes, they even get a parting gift, maybe a plaque or a personalized soldier statue. I've been to some where they gave them a sword, a gift basket, a signed picture frame, or a simple card, at the very least. If nothing else, a Hail and Farewell is a heartfelt time when your colleagues and bosses honor soldiers and share what an asset they were, or how they always brightened the workplace, and how they are sad to see them go. Colleagues might tell a funny story involving your shenanigans or shed a tear or two as they honor you. It's the rule more than the exception that soldiers are presented with an Army award.

Farewells & Forgiveness

Although I wasn't holding my breath that Chaplain Eagle would, I assumed one of the soldiers in my unit would at least have people meet together for lunch with me at the food court on post. I realized, as my time dwindled down and after I out processed and was on terminal leave, a Hail and Farewell was not in the cards for me. Sergeant Carr said she was too busy and hadn't been here long, and from what she had seen, I hadn't done anything worthy of an award, but if I felt I deserved one, I had to write it up. Most NCOs write their awards (this is true), and she said, reluctantly, she would sign it. So I did. I sent the evidence to justify an award, and she turned it in to the unit. My award was submitted but was downgraded from a nicer award that typically accompanies an ETS or PCS, from an Army accommodation to an Army achievement award. Remembering that all left in our unit was me, and the four others were sergeants that were chaplain assistants, remembering that Chaplain who just wanted my head on a platter, I hoped that one of the sergeants would fight for me to get my award and my Hail and Farewell. I have always been someone who has felt my character could stand on its own, and despite everything, they saw I did my job and cared for the people I served.

My official last day of boots on the ground came and went. I was out of the Army. I had so many vacation days that I was able to exit in July, although my official ETS day wasn't until September.

One day in August, I waited for Stephen to come home for lunch. Startled by the knocking on my apartment door, I opened it, and Sergeant Church stood there in his civilian clothes. He handed me a green certificate folder. "Specialist Hayes, here's your award." My jaw dropped open.

"Sergeant?"

"Sorry it's this way, but you are lucky that you even got this. I had to fight for this for you."

This was the Army, and it was my unit's last chance to show they cared. This was my unit's chance to show they valued my time, my service, and my contribution, but all they said in actions was, "Don't let the door hit ya where the good Lord split ya."

When I look back on it, I believe that sometimes people who are not bad people are compliant with bad behavior. They don't know how to stand up for what is right, or they are scared. They don't want to make waves, they don't want that negative attention to be turned onto them, and they don't want to put a target on their backs. I think the lack of experience, lack of understanding, and fear makes people scared to stand up to someone like Chaplain Eagle, or anyone else in a position of power. I used to think that people could be neutral in not wanting to get involved. It's uncomfortable, but now I think of inaction as a stance. We should hold each other accountable for ethical and moral treatment.

Most of the chaplain assistants were young, in their late teens, twenties, and early thirties. I am able to feel thankful for the lessons I learned, the strengthening of my relationship, and learning to speak truth, no matter what is at stake. That's not to say it didn't hurt. Regardless of the lessons I am now thankful for, I was not thankful in that moment. I felt as if I had the worst breakup in my life. I was leaving the Army, and not being able to deploy with the brigade made my heart sink. Those people were my friends and my mentors, my support. I wasn't sure if mint chocolate chip ice cream and prayer could fix this one.

God help me to forgive. I don't want to be bitter! This would end up being my rally cry. They say time heals all wounds, but I would argue that isn't true. If I never dealt with the loss and the hurt, I wouldn't be able to heal. If a person does not do that hard work of forgiveness, then bitterness and resentment will take root.

I did, however, learn through time that forgiveness is not for the offenders, but for those affected. It is balm for our soul and peace for our health. I believe God calls us to forgive and, when possible and healthy, reconcile, and when it's toxic or not possible, to release it. Over time, I learned to forgive. I needed to forgive because as people, we never, never forget. It was almost harder to forgive Chaplain Eagle and Sergeant Church than the soldier who had assaulted me because the offense was also toward my husband. I felt as if, by forgiving them, I was excusing bad behavior. However, forgiveness does not mean accepting injustices or taking a vow of silence and letting our offenders off the hook. One of my favorite verses says to "love mercy, pursue justice and walk humbly with God." When we hold on to bitterness, resentment, or hurt, it takes a physical toll on our bodies. It can shave years off our lives, cause problems from stress, and take up mental space. So, I had to make a choice. I had to forgive. It was a process. In fact, it is still a process. I forgave years ago, and when those feelings are dredged up again, because they sometimes are, it's a matter of choosing to forgive again, and again. I have to continually ask myself whether I wanted to get better or stay bitter.

The brigade chaplain and chaplain assistant, Chaplain Staff and Sergeant Drum, heard from my husband that the unit didn't have a farewell for me. They decided to add me in on one of their celebrations. The chaplains and chaplain assistants who cared about me along the way became lifelong friends, and they helped me end my Army career feeling as if some of my comrades cared. They invited me to their function to honor me. Tears filled my eyes, as they told me how they saw me and appreciated my efforts. That is all that I wanted, anyway—acknowledgment and gratitude. Those words spoke life to me. Those soldiers and their families were my family. They loved me. The last thing I was standing on was my reputation, and to not have it acknowledged by my own unit felt like a low blow. I had to face myself. What was I helping people for? What was I doing my job for? If I was working for men's approval, I wasn't getting that from my unit. Being honored by the brigade softened the blow, but it still hurt that my own team didn't value me. Sergeant Whisk, the sergeant who caught me sneaking snacks in my training, was there. He was stationed in Anchorage and had come up to check on all the chaplain assistants in Fairbanks, as we fall under the Pacific command, including all of Alaska and Hawaii. His eyes sparkled mischievously, as he made his way to me.

"Still love gummy worms?"

"Ha, Sergeant. I actually prefer the bears."

"Hey, and congrats on your wedding! We love when chaplain assistants get together! It's a beautiful thing, love. We were surprised no one told us anything. If we had known about your wedding, we would have at least sent a card."

"It's a long story, Sergeant, maybe for another time."

Humans will let you down. It's just a part of life. I realized when I used my gifts to serve and love well, I had done my job, imperfectly, but with empathy and to the best of my ability. I worked for the families that were being counseled, the families and units that thanked us after the twentieth memorial, the soldier or spouse who just needed an ear because life overwhelmed them. I did it for the mom who lost her baby and needed to talk to me because she was sure the unmarried chaplain in her unit just didn't understand. I did it for the soldier whose unit was not helping as he struggled with suicidal ideology and self-harm from depression and undiagnosed symptoms of PTSD. I came alongside and held their hands. I prayed with them. I led them to Chaplain Sword and drove them to the mental health facility when they wanted to end it all. I encouraged and loved people. This is not to pat myself on the back; I did my job, and that was my duty. I wanted to help people. I wanted to make a difference.

Sometimes, I still struggle with not deploying and whether I truly am worthy of the word veteran. But I know I did my part. I fulfilled my assignment and my purpose during those years. I needed to remind myself that I don't do these things for the applause of others. They may or may not recognize me. When I joined the Army, I chose my job as a chaplain assistant because I wanted to help the crushed and brokenhearted, and I wanted to give hope to the hopeless. I craved getting words of affirmation and recognition, but with or without them, I fulfilled the calling God gave me. I ended my four-year Army career with a Good Conduct Medal, a driver's badge, four Army Achievement Medals, and quite a few certificates of achievement and appreciation.

I ended my Army time finding connection, friends, and most importantly, the love of my life. I grew into the woman I am today, and I am still growing into a woman who will stand up for herself and others. Those "other" awards that the Army gave me will never be able to be quantified on a plaque or displayed on my wall. Despite my earlier doubt in myself, despite what plans I thought I had for my Army career, it was over. I could breathe easy.

Free at last. Stephen and I were married and still in love. We had gone through the fire and come out refined. I reconciled with God. I didn't understand, and I didn't appreciate it in the middle of the storm, but God used our broken parts and made something beautiful. I knew that if Stephen and I survived all that we had gone through, we could make it. We could make it through this deployment. We could make it through anything.

Epilogue

Years went by, and Church's wife found and befriended me on social media through mutual friends. I don't know why I connected with her, but she was sweet, and I felt like it was okay to do so. I had written parts of our story on social media about the importance of anti-racist work. Church's wife commented on my post about her husband being an advocate for Stephen, and I was shocked! Through her eyes, Church had fought for us.

What on Earth is she talking about? I wrote a private message to her.

"I'm not trying to be rude, and I don't know what you heard, but from my experience, I didn't see it like that."

She was surprised and told her husband, and he reached out to me, asking if we could talk. He wasn't the hero in my story, but I agreed

Epilogue

to hear him out. I was curious because of his wife's comments of what his story was. How did he see our time working together?

I had forgiven him years ago, but it felt good to have him apologize for the pain and lack of standing up for us. It felt good for the acknowledgement and some type of closure. I know people aren't always able to reconcile, but for him to care enough to listen and then have him share what was going on, on his end, was a relief. According to Church, he didn't know about the legal things Chaplain Eagle was pushing. He told me he had tried to stand up for us at times, but he admitted he was young and foolish, and he failed us as a leader. He said if he could go back, he would have done things differently. He regretted his inaction and asked for forgiveness. I had already forgiven him, but I had a sense of relief wash over me, as Church made amends with me. While we may never be best friends, we are amiable. Church became a professional reference for me for job opportunities and higher education. God can redeem anything or anyone, and my life is the proof of that.

Acknowledgments

Stephen- You are my best friend and love of my life. Thank you for believing me and encouraging me, even when I didn't believe in myself. From the time I met you until now, you have shown me patience, grace and have been the source of unconditional love. Living life by your side has been an adventure from the very start. Thank you for allowing me to peek into what it is like to walk in your shoes and share our story freely. Thank you for helping with the cover and dealing with me changing my mind. I love you more.

For my children- I could never explain how you guys fuel me to try and do better. Please don't ever let someone define you based on your skin color, your hair, or anything about who you are. You are enough. You are made in God's image, each one of you are perfectly designed with your unique characteristics. I pray you know how much of an honor and joy it is to parent you. Even when you drive me crazy by calling, "mom, mommy, ma," 1000 times, I cherish that title immensely. I love you all.

Brenita and Lianne- Thank you for being my biggest cheerleaders and encouraging me every single step along the way. Thanks for having my six. I couldn't ask for better sisters. I love you both!

Mom and Dad- Thank you for showing me how to love others, and always showing me that good people can make a difference. Thank you for showing me to look at people and love based on the content of their character, not based on their outside appearance. Thank you for loving Stephen and my kids. I wish all families were as supportive. I love you.

For my Army family that loved and supported us, I am humbled to have served with you and grateful for you all.

For my extended family, thank you for loving Stephen, me and the kids so well, and being there for me.

Thank you to all my melaninated family and friends. I can never fully grasp it all, but the injustice you face on the daily and the love you still pour out, despite being tired, it is astounding. I marvel at the strength, dignity, power and resiliency you have shown in your lives and in the stories you entrusted to me. I promise to keep learning and doing better, and to link arms with you to not only pursue equality and justice, but equity.

For my editors- Emily K. Thank you for taking my very rough first draft and helping me develop it. Danielle Anderson- Thank you for your time and effort. Thank you for the support in helping me pull together my story. Thank you for the community you created and the conference calls and sharing your plethora of knowledge. I am so grateful for you. .

Last but not least-Thank you Lord for your forgiveness so I can forgive others. Thank you for your grace so that I can be gracious to others and your unconditional love. Thank you for redeeming my story. I'm so grateful for you turning my pain into purpose, and my grief into glory. I pray that my story brings awareness and healing, but most of all I want to give you all the credit for working in my life.

CAMOUFLAGED LOVE

Veteran Women Resources

WoVeN

https://www.wovenwomenvets.org

WoVeN is a vibrant community for women Veterans of all eras and service branches. In addition to providing community, WoVeN strives to empower women Veterans with information, education, and resources to improve their quality of life

The Pink Berets

httpss://thepinkberets.org

Mission is to educate, coordinate, and provide aid and relief to active duty women of the U.S. and Veterans seeking assistance with invisible injuries such as Post Traumatic Stress Disorder, Military Sexual Trauma and Combat Trauma Stress on a local and national level

Wounded Warrior Project

https://woundedwarriorproject.org

Veterans and service members who incurred a physical or mental injury, illness, or wound while serving in the military on or after September 11, 2001. You are our focus. community mental wellness, physical wellness, career and VA counseling, independent program.

Texas Veterans:
https://www.texvet.org/women-veterans

Military Rape Crisis Center 1-877-995-5247
The Military Rape Crisis Center (MRCC) strives to unite agencies engaged in the elimination of sexual violence in the United States Armed Forces. MRCC provides case management, victim advocacy, support groups, education, research, and training.

Veterans Crisis Line 1-800-273-8255
The Veterans Crisis Line connects Veterans in crisis and their families and friends with qualified, caring Department of Veterans Affairs responders through a confidential toll-free hotline, online chat, or text.

Vets for Warriors 1-855-838-8255
Vets4Warriors'peer-to-peer support network connects people, information, ideas and resources to generate powerful solutions for members of the military and veteran communities. They are 100% staffed by trained veterans and members of the military community, their families or caregivers.

VA women hotline 1-855-829-6636

Crisis Hotlines
NVF Lifeline for Vets – 1-888-777-4443
VA Suicide Hotline – 1-800-273-8255
National Suicide Hotline - 1-800-273-TALK (8255)
Stop Soldier Suicide - 1-800-273-8255 #1

Antiracism Resources

https://www.pbssocal.org/education/how-to-talk-to-your-kids-about-anti-racism-a-list-of-resources

https://www.antiracismproject.org/resources

https://nymag.com/strategist/article/anti-racist-reading-list.html

https://www.penguinrandomhouse.com/articles/anti-racist-books-and-resources

https://bethebridge.com

https://www.austinchanning.com

https://www.ibramxkendi.com

https://blackhistoryintwominutes.com

Podcast-Scene on Radio: Seeing White
https://www.sceneonradio.org/seeing-white

CAMOUFLAGED LOVE

About the Author

Lorin Hayes is the author of Camouflaged Love. Her experience as an Army soldier and then as a spouse for the duration of her husband's Army career, until he retired, increased her desire to help others navigate life's obstacles.

Lorin completed a degree in Psychology with a minor in Christian Counseling and holds a certification in professional life coaching. She resides in Texas with her husband, and four children.

She loves spending time with her family, at church and community programs, cooking together, playing sports or family game nights. Some nights she can be found relaxing with her favorite honey chamomile tea curled up with a book.

Find more about Lorin @ www.lorinhayes.com or connect via Facebook, and Instagram @authorlorinhayes.

Made in the USA
Columbia, SC
26 August 2021